All About Mancala

Its History and How to Play

Sue and Jon Hanson

Sue Hanson

Jon Hanson

Published by
Happy Viking Crafts
Mahomet, IL

All About Mancala

Its History and How to Play

Sue and Jon Hanson

Published by:
>   Happy Viking Crafts
>   Mahomet, IL 61853

Manufactured in the United States of America

Publisher's Cataloging in Publication

Hanson, Sue.
>   All about mancala: its history and how to play / Sue and Jon Hanson ; with photographs and illustrations.--1st ed.
>   p. cm.
>   Includes bibliographical references and index.
>   LCCN 2003105182
>   ISBN 0-9740175-0-7
1. Mancala (Games) 2. Mancala (Games) - History. I. Jon Hanson. II. Title.
GV1469 2003
794.2—DC21

We dedicate this book to
the original Happy Viking, Charles Hanson.

TABLE OF CONTENTS

PREFACE

LIKE MANY SMALL craft businesses, ours started as a living room conversation. We thought it might be fun to make and sell crafts. So back in 1990, along with Jon's parents, we found a site at the Bristol Renaissance Faire in Wisconsin. There we built a booth and started a business called Happy Viking Crafts. We have been there ever since.

We were interested in historical board games, so along with a variety of other hand-made crafts, we sold Tick-tack-toe, Fox and Geese, and Nine-men's Morris. All were made of quality hardwoods such as oak and walnut and used marbles for playing pieces. To us, each was a unique bit of history. (Sadly, this wasn't always obvious to our customers who too often commented, "Look, it's Chinese Checkers!" to everything we had on the counter. How anyone can think Tick-tack-toe is Chinese Checkers remains a mystery to all of us at Happy Viking.)

When we put our first games out for sale, we had never heard of mancala or any of its relatives. Our first encounter with this game was a customer who came to our booth looking for a game called Wari. It was from Africa, she said. It sounded interesting and fit our theme of historical games, so we headed for the library. Surprisingly, though, we found little written on Wari. It was only after extensive searching that we finally located basic instructions in an out-of-print game book from a used bookstore.

When we first read the instructions for Wari, we were rather confused. Unlike most games we had played, you did not own the pieces nor did the pieces have any value. All you did was pick them up and drop them one by one into holes arranged in rows. However, as we played Wari, it began to make more sense. We could see that it was very mathematical and that it had a great deal of strategy. Between players of equal ability, it was no easy task to win. We decided Wari was a good game to add to our line of products.

When we first offered Wari at Happy Viking, we were amazed at the response. We had no idea so many Americans were interested in the game. Many had seen it and wanted to learn it or remembered it from childhood and wanted to play it again. Others were avid fans and were thrilled finally to find the game for which they had been looking so long.

We offered to play Wari with these folks. Surprisingly, though, few of them played by the rules we had learned from our game book. Instead, most people played by another set of rules, and they called the game "mancala". (From here on, we will call this game "Cross Capture Mancala" and use "mancala" to mean the family of games.) Cross Capture Mancala was similar to Wari in some ways, but plays were made through the reservoir and the style of capturing was different.

At first, we thought there was only one set of rules for Cross Capture Mancala, but as we played more customers, we saw that it had many variations. Jon wrote down each one he encountered. Many proved to be only slight variations of the "standard" game, but some were quite different. It was obvious that Cross Capture Mancala was evolving in the United States just as it had in Africa.

While we found Cross Capture Mancala was the standard among American players, we were surprised to find that among our foreign customers it was not. In fact, they often played versions that did not resemble Cross Capture Mancala at all. This sparked my (Sue's) curiosity and I headed back to the library where I searched out every game of mancala I could find. Adding these to what Jon had documented, we ended up with quite a collection of games, each unique. Different types of gameboards were used as well as different styles of capturing. There were many interesting twists added to games, such as secondary capturing and different endings. How such a game could have so many versions, yet so clearly remain mancala seemed amazing.

Over time, we added some of the more interesting versions to our line of products. We were pleased that our customers showed an interest in them, although I think Cross Capture Mancala will never lose its place as the all-American favorite. As you might expect, we later developed a few versions of our own. The most notable of these is a four-person game called Crossroads Mancala, which is based on Cross Capture Mancala.

When we started our business, we never thought we would be writing a book on mancala. In fact, the beginnings of this book were little more than a double-sided sheet of instructions to go with our original "Wari" game. The sheet contained the standard game of Cross Capture Mancala, four variations we had learned from our customers, plus Wari.

Soon, however, the double-sided sheet became inadequate. Although it outlined the basics on how to play, customers came back with questions. Other customers complained that they were unable to find any mancala instructions from other sources. It was clear that something better was needed. Therefore, we added some detail to our two-sided sheet and made it look more professional. The result was a booklet called *Mancala Mania: Sampler, Six American Favorites*.

Sampler was a great success, so when we added other mancala games to our line of products, we also produced instruction booklets for them. They became part of the *Mancala Mania* series and included *Sungka: Filipino Mancala; Pallanguli: Indian Mancala; Four-Row: Eastern \African Mancala;* and finally *Crossroads: Mancala for Four*. Again, this was not enough. Customers now wanted a complete book containing all the games.

Writing a complete book on mancala proved to be a far bigger undertaking than we expected, however. We had enough games, but finding information on the history and culture of mancala - especially the forms played outside of western Africa and the United States - was difficult. In addition, we had to play each game we wanted to include to be sure it played well. It was surprising how many games did not, even documented games. A rule was missing or poorly explained, or one player might have too much of an advantage. We had to modify these games so they would be playable, but not too much or they would lose their original flavor.

Then there was figuring out the strategy. To comment on this subject, we had to understand how each game was won. This involved playing many times, trying not to confuse the rules of the current game with the last one. It was during this phase that we really became convinced that even the slightest change to the rules in mancala could greatly impact the strategy and make it a whole new game.

So, we got our start in mancala almost by accident. We started with a customer's request for a game called Wari, and ended up writing a book. We feel lucky to have been on the ground floor of recent American interest in mancala and have enjoyed growing with it. It will be interesting to see what will happen next.

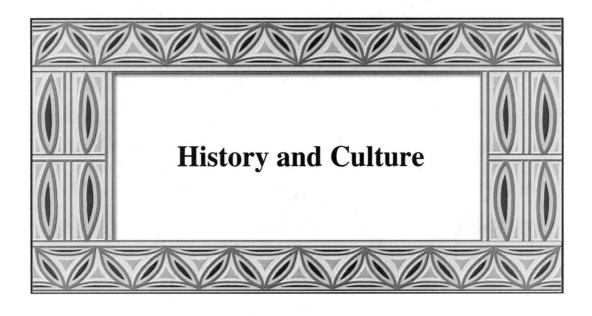

History and Culture

**Author and daughter playing Hus on a four-row
board made by authors.**

THE HISTORY OF MANCALA

MANCALA IS THE name of a family of similar boardgames believed to have originated in Ancient Egypt. It is one of the oldest boardgames in existence and has been played for thousands of years. It is also one of the most widespread games, being found all over the world. Mancala has been played for centuries in the Middle East, India, and Southeast Asia. More recently, it has found its way to Europe, the United States, and parts of the Caribbean and South America. However, the place where mancala has been played the longest and is the most popular is Africa. There it is played throughout the continent and is considered Africa's National Game.

Because it is so widespread, mancala has many variations. Despite this, though, all mancala games have certain basic characteristics in common. First, they are games for two players (although a few forms exist for three and four players). Second, they are played on a gameboard consisting of two to four long rows of hollows or cups. The gameboard is placed between the two players such that each faces the long rows of cups. Third, at the beginning of the game, the cups are filled with playing pieces, such as seeds or stones. Players pick up the playing pieces and redistribute or sow them around the board according to a set of rules. Their intent is to capture the stones as they are sown. Either the number of stones captured or leaving your opponent no possible plays determines the winner.

WHERE MANCALA ORIGINATED

Mancala is known to date back at least 1400 years before the birth of Christ but may have been in existence long before that. Precisely where it originated, though, is difficult to say, as few records have survived. Most historians believe mancala originated in Egypt. Relic gameboards have been found among the ancient Egyptian ruins, and Egypt has been the source of many other ancient games. A few historians, however, believe that mancala originated in Sumeria, a part of ancient Mesopotamia located in what is today southern Iraq. These historians maintain that Arab traders subsequently brought the game to Egypt and other parts of Africa.

Another theory is that mancala originated in another part of Africa and was later introduced to Egypt and the Middle East. This theory is based on the fact that mancala games are very widespread in Africa and there are so many different versions. In addition, some of these versions, such as the four-row games of eastern and southern Africa, are unique and do not appear to have ever been played elsewhere.

As interesting as they are, any theories that mancala originated outside of Egypt have been difficult to prove, however. No written records have survived if, indeed, there ever were any. In addition, while ancient gameboards have been found in the Middle East, Zimbabwe, Ghana, Uganda, and Ethiopia, none predate those found in Egypt.

HOW MANCALA ORIGINATED

Like most ancient games, mancala probably did not start as a game. More likely, it had another purpose. What this purpose was, though, historians can only guess. One theory is that mancala started as a record keeping system. The Sumerians, a civilization of about the third millennium BC, were among the first peoples to keep accurate numerical records. They may have used mancala as a counting tool in the same way the Chinese used the abacus. The counting nature of this game lends credence to this theory.

Another theory is that mancala was originally associated with a ritual. Over time, the ritual was forgotten and only the game remained. Many ancient games played today started this way. For instance, the modern children's game of Jacks evolved from an ancient fortune telling ritual that involved the tossing of sheep's knucklebones. (An interesting contrast, the gambling game of Craps also evolved from this ritual.)

Unfortunately, because so little evidence has survived, any ritual associated with mancala can only be speculated on. However, there are a few theories. One is that mancala started as part of a spring planting ritual. The outcome of the game was interpreted as a message from the gods regarding the harvest. Evidence to support this theory is that in many African societies a farming association is made with mancala. The cups on the gameboard represent fields. The playing pieces, usually seeds themselves, are the seeds that are sown into the fields. The circular motion of sowing represents the seasons of planting and harvesting. The capturing of pieces represents crops brought in at harvest time.

Gameboards found at African shrines and temples suggest a different ritual may have once been associated with mancala. At a temple in Nigeria, this ritual is still known. The gameboard represents the world. The stones are the stars, and the cups, the months of the year. When used, the gameboard is laid east to west, so that it is in alignment with the rising and setting sun. Moving the stones represents the gods moving through time and space. In this way, mancala predicts our fate. However, since we can choose which stones to move, mancala also teaches us that we can control our world.

There are other rituals associated with mancala besides these. They occur not only in Africa but in other parts of the world as well. An interesting coincidence is the similarity of some of these rituals, suggesting they may have had a common source.

MANCALA BECOMES A GAME

Wherever and however mancala originated, by 1400 BC it was being used in Egypt as a game. Attesting to this is a number of gameboards found carved into certain ancient Egyptian ruins. Among the oldest gameboards are several that were carved into the roofing slabs of the Temple of Kurna, built around 1400 BC in ancient Thebes. Mancala gameboards have also been found carved into a pylon at the entrance of the temple at Karnak, near Thebes. This temple was built during the three centuries before Christ.

It could be argued that these gameboards were carved into the monuments long after they were built. However, historians do not think this is the case. The reason is that parts of the gameboards were cut away when the stones were placed and fitted. Historians thus speculate that stone masons building the monuments carved these games for their playing enjoyment while the stones were still on the ground.

It is unfortunate that so many of these gameboards are incomplete. However, enough parts remain to give an idea of what the gameboards originally looked like. By comparing them with modern gameboards, historians have a better idea of how mancala might have once been played.

4

MANCALA SPREADS FROM EGYPT

To Africa and Asia

Games were a popular pastime in the Mediterranean at the time of ancient Egypt, and it was not long before mancala began to spread. It first spread to the nearby areas of Africa and the Middle East with whom Egypt had trade relations. Evidence for this is that versions played in these areas today are very similar. In addition, many of the names used for mancala appear to be derivations of the Egyptian name for the game Mankala'h. Some examples are Mancal in Ethiopia, Magala in Sudan, and Kalah in the Middle East. Finally, mancala gameboards that predate Islam have been found in the Middle East. This means that mancala was played there before 600 AD.

By 600 AD, mancala was well established in the Middle East and began to spread further eastward into Asia. It was first spread by Muslim conquerors who are believed to have introduced mancala to India, at the eastern end of their empire. How or when the game arrived in Southeast Asia is not clear. However, it may have been brought there by Muslims as well or been introduced by Indian and African traders.

To Europe

Although Mancala spread quite early to Africa and Asia, it did not make its way to Europe until centuries later. In fact, mancala was little known in Europe until the 19th century. This is surprising since the Romans, Vikings, Moors, and later the Crusaders introduced Europe to so many other ancient games from Africa and Asia including chess, checkers, and backgammon. However, if mancala was among these games, it was either ignored or forgotten. It was not until the 1800s when they were colonizing Africa that Europeans really became aware of mancala.

Even then, Europeans did not give mancala much attention. The game baffled them, probably because it was played so differently from the games they were familiar with. In addition, they considered the Africans primitive, so ignored mancala as a trivial native pastime.

The European attitude toward mancala changed somewhat in the 19th century due to the work of Edward Lane, an Englishman who lived in Cairo during the 1830s. Lane was interested in the Egyptian way of life. Among the things he studied were their forms of recreation. He found an unusual game played at Cairo's coffeehouses. The game was called Mankala'h. It was a social game, and the loser had to pay for the coffee. Lane learned the game and produced the first written description of a mancala game. Lane's work subsequently popularized the name "mancala" that is used today to describe the family of games.

Since Lane, other European sociologists have looked more closely at mancala. They have been intrigued by the numerous versions and even more so by the social customs associated with the game. They have published their findings, although somewhat sporadically, in articles and books. However, in spite of their interest, Europeans have never had the attraction to mancala that other cultures have. This fact is alluded to in some of the articles written about mancala during the early 20th century. One comments that Europeans have considerable interest in learning the variations of mancala but far less in actually playing the game.

To the Caribbean and South America

Mancala was introduced to the New World during the time of the slave trade when large numbers of Africans were brought in to work the plantations. Although they worked as slaves, they kept the parts of their culture that they could and this included the games they played. Because of this, mancala became well established in many parts of the New World. Some of the most notable areas are the Caribbean and the eastern coast of South America.

Several forms of mancala have been found in the New World, but the most common is a western African version known generally as Wari. There are several documented variations of Wari played in the Caribbean, and many more undocumented variations. They have remained essentially unchanged since the days the earliest Africans arrived. In fact, it has been possible to trace the roots of the descendents of these Africans by studying the variation of Wari they play. Wari is also found in South America where, again, it remains little changed. In British Guyana, children still play in holes carved in the dirt using stones or pieces of burnt peat as playing pieces just as their ancestors did.

While Wari is the prevalent form of mancala found in the New World, other versions are played as well. Some appear to be New World developments, as they are not related to any known games of the Old World.

To the United States

The Africans brought in as slaves also introduced mancala to the United States, which was again most likely a version of Wari. Gameboards have been found in excavations of slave quarters and residences near such places as historic Yorktown in Virginia. However, Wari (and therefore mancala) remained little known outside Black culture for many decades. In fact, to some degree it was suppressed, as White society of that time disapproved of African forms of recreation.

The attitude toward mancala changed in the 1890s, when a group of Syrian immigrants living in New York introduced their version of mancala called Chuba. Americans were very interested in new and different board games at this time, and Chuba became all the rage.

In 1891, Milton Bradley produced the first commercially manufactured game of mancala. It was named *Chuba* after the prototype. In the 1900s, other commercial games of mancala were manufactured. One of these was *Kalah*, designed by William Champion and manufactured by Kalah, Inc. In the 1950s, *Pitfall* was produced by Creative Playthings. In the 1960s, *Oh-Wah-Ree* was put out by 3M. Today mancala is widely available from any department store. It is also available on computer either as commercially sold software or via Internet downloads.

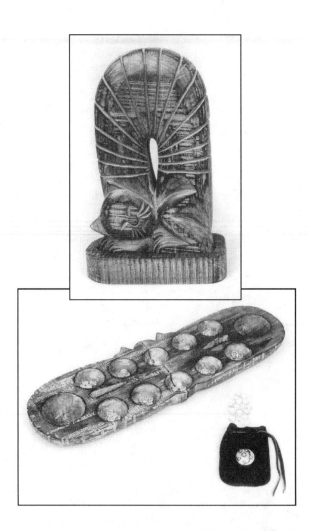

**Folding Indonesian animal figure board from authors'
collection.**

THE CULTURE OF MANCALA

WHO MAY PLAY MANCALA

Playing conventions are the unwritten rules a society has for playing a game. They set the guidelines for who may play, when they may play, and even who may construct the gameboard. Regarding mancala, playing conventions vary considerably. In the United States and Europe, for instance, they are very relaxed. Mancala is played for recreation and anyone may play at any time or place. However, in other societies there are strict playing conventions. This is especially the case where mancala has been played for many centuries.

In parts of Africa, mancala was once reserved only for royalty and people of rank. For instance, when Uganda was a monarchy, mancala was part of the ritual associated with the crowning of a new king. It was also used for deciding the outcome of court cases. Therefore, it was considered too important to be used as a game by the common people.

Today such class restrictions regarding mancala have mostly disappeared, but conventions regarding which sex may play still exist. In some parts of Africa (and African settlements in the Caribbean), mancala is strictly a man's game. It is not considered proper for women to play, one of the prevalent reasons being women are too busy with their work. To discourage them from playing, women are warned if they do, there will be a terrible outcome. For example, in one society, they are told if they touch a mancala board, the crops will not grow. In another, girls are told if they play mancala, they will not develop into women and no one will marry them.

Fortunately, most African societies are not this restrictive. Women are allowed to play mancala, although they must play simple children's versions and only with each other. They must never excel, however, or they will be dully chided. Of course, some women excel anyway, but men will not play them. For a man to lose to a woman is considered socially humiliating.

Like class restrictions, restrictions based on sex appear to be changing. In Zaire, some of the older women have become champions at a version of mancala called Tshisolo. The men have tried to stop them, but they have not been successful.

It is interesting to note that while many African societies consider mancala a man's game, in southern India and Sri Lanka it is considered a woman's game. Women play for recreation after the morning chores are finished. Men are not restricted from playing, but they seldom play mancala except for gambling purposes.

WHEN MANCALA MAY BE PLAYED

In some societies there are conventions determining when mancala may be played. For instance, in the Philippines, mancala is traditionally only played at funerals. This keeps the spirit of the deceased amused until it departs for the next world. The game must be put away at sundown, however, and it must be stored away from the house, or it will bring bad luck to the owner. Judging from the number of Filipino players we have met who are avid mancala players, though, it does not appear that this convention is taken too seriously.

In Central America, there is a similar convention. When a man of the village dies, villagers play mancala in the house of mourning to amuse his spirit until after the funeral. However, the game is only played during the day, because after dark other spirits may join in and carry off the souls of the living players. There are no restrictions on playing at other times, however. This is because the village keeps two boards, one flat and one curved. After the funeral, the board in use is put away and the other brought out for playing. In this way, the deceased will not recognize the board and join the living players.

Some societies have conventions governing who may construct a mancala board. For instance, in Central America it is bad luck for anyone except an old man who has lost a wife to carve a new gameboard. He will deliberately make the board crude and imperfect, however. It is bad luck for anyone but the players to smooth the unfinished cups. (Having sanded many mancala cups at Happy Viking, we suspect there is an ulterior motive to this last convention.)

STORIES AND LEGENDS

In some areas, especially in Africa, wonderful stories and legends are associated with mancala. In northern Kenya, before the lion goes on a hunt, he is said to dig holes in the sand and play mancala. If the game goes well, his hunting will also go well. If the game goes poorly, his hunting will go poorly.

An equally interesting legend, and one that has a historical basis, is told in Zaire. Four hundred years ago, there was a king known as Shamba Bolongongo who ruled the Kuba people. He wanted his people to stop fighting and spend more time improving themselves and the village. One of the things he did was to introduce mancala, a game that could teach them peaceful ways.

THE ART OF THE GAMEBOARD

Gameboard implies a construction of wood, but not all mancala gameboards are made of wood. In actuality, a variety of materials are used. It all depends on what is available to players, what they like, and what they can afford.

The simplest mancala gameboards are made of materials that are cheap and easily available. In many African societies and those of African descent, children dig mancala boards in the dirt. African herders and nomadic peoples, especially those who live in dry climates, carve gameboards into a convenient stone. In the United States, children use muffin tins and egg cartons to play.

At the other extreme are mancala boards made of precious materials, being meant for use by royalty and the affluent. The Asante kings of Africa, for instance, once used boards made of gold. The wealthy of India once used boards of carved ivory. A rather unusual board, also made in India, was composed of metal with chromium plate. Today gameboards intended for sale to collectors are sometimes made of quality stone such as marble.

While a variety of materials is used for making mancala gameboards, the majority of boards are of wood. Many are simple constructions, being intended for everyday use. Some, though, are quite elaborate, especially in societies where mancala is highly regarded.

In Africa, for example, mancala boards are often made of special hardwoods with traditional shapes and figures carved into them. Some are further decorated with shells, inlayed wood, or silver. In India and Southeast Asia, gameboards are carved into special shapes such as boats or abstracts of animals. In the United States, while wooden gameboards are kept simple in design, they are sometimes decorated by layering woods or adding wood inlays.

Where mancala is important, gameboards are highly valued. For instance, in the Philippines, gameboards are handed down from parent to child, some for many generations. In some African societies and societies of African descent there is a village gameboard. It is constructed following a special set of rules and once made is highly valued and used for many years.

A FAMILY OF GAMES

Mancala is a family of games, and its descendents and offshoots make up hundreds of variations. At least two hundred have been documented, and it is speculated that there are hundreds more beyond that. That so many variations of a single game could exist leads to a basic question. How did this occur?

This question in itself is a subject worthy of detailed study. However, on a general level, there are some answers. For one thing, mancala is very ancient and has been played by many people. Until recently, the only way it was taught was by word of mouth. Even in the United States, until recent interest spawned so much documentation (including on the internet) most players learned mancala from a friend or through a social institution such as school or scouts. Word of mouth introduces changes. A rule is misunderstood or forgotten. A game is modified to make it simpler for beginners or more challenging for experienced players. A different method of playing, possibly influenced by another game, is added. Such changes are minor when considered individually. However, when multiplied by thousands of people over thousands of years, it is not surprising that there are so many variations of mancala.

Second, mancala is mathematically based, and its rules can be added to, modified, or recombined in a myriad of ways. For instance, you can start the game with three stones per cup instead of four. You can end the game when your side of the board goes empty of stones or your opponent's side goes empty of stones. You can also change the rules regarding capturing, choosing to capture cups holding two stones rather than three or a loaded cup opposite an empty cup. The list goes on and on, and like a mathematical formula, each change to the rules creates a different "problem" with its own solution. Counting the combinations and permutations of possible changes to the rules, the result is hundreds of ways to play.

Interestingly, no matter how small the change, there is nearly always an effect on the strategy. This effect may be small, such as occurs when starting the game with three rather than four stones per cup. It may be more significant, such as changing the ending would be. In some cases, though, a change to the rules may result in an entirely different version of the game. This is especially true when there has been a change to the object or method of capturing.

A MYRIAD OF NAMES

With so many variations of mancala among so many cultures, you can well imagine that there is a myriad of names for this game. This leads to a second question, which name is correct? In the same way that there is no single way to play mancala, there is no single correct name. The name used depends entirely on who is playing the game and where.

In the United States, mancala has been known by a number of names. Some of these have been adopted from the ethnic name for a particular version. Chuba and Kalah from the Middle East and Wari and Adi from Africa are two examples. Others have been colloquial names such as Pits and Stones, the African Stone Game, and even the Park District Game. With the exception of Wari, however, these names are mostly obsolete. Most Americans refer to the game by the name for the family of related games, "mancala". This is probably due to the influence of commercial game companies that have made this name a standard.

As in the United States, other cultures have their particular name or names for mancala. The list is exhaustive, but following are a few of the more interesting ones. In Egypt the game is known as Mankala'h. In the Middle East, it is called Kalah or Chuba. In India, mancala is known as Pallanguli, Parchgarhwa and Kutaboia. In the Philippines, it is called Sungka and Chungkajohn. In Africa where it is so widespread, mancala has more names than any other place in the world, at least one and sometimes several for nearly every tribe that plays it. These names include among others Wari, Warri, Wouri, Aware, Adi, and Asante, which are used in northern and western Africa. In eastern and southern Africa where four-row mancala is played, variations are known by such names as Bare', Hus, Omweso, and a real tongue twister, Bao Kiswahili Bao Bau.

Names for the variations of mancala are so numerous and diverse that they appear to have nothing in common. However, an interesting consistency among them is that they usually describe some element of the game. The Philippine name Sungka and Ugandan name Omweso, for instance, refer to the gameboard. The Nigerian name Adi refers to the aditi bush from which the seeds for playing are obtained. The American name, Pits and Stones, refers to both the gameboard and playing pieces.

In other cases, the name refers to some element of playing the game. The Egyptian name Mankala'h, for instance, refers to the action taken to play. It comes from an Arabic word *manqala*, that in turn comes from the verb *naqala* meaning, "to move" as in moving the playing pieces. There are also games where the name refers to its level of difficulty. In Nigeria, there is a form of mancala called Ise-Ozin-Egbe, which translates as the "Perseverance Game".

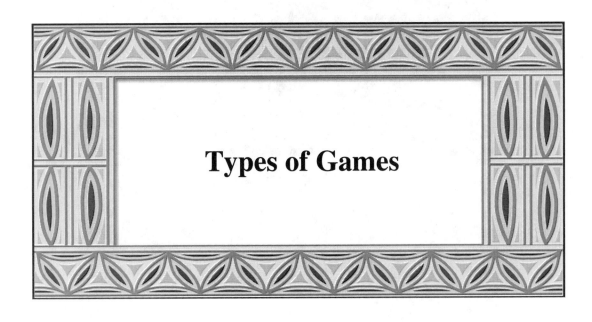

Types of Games

Author making different types of mancala boards.

THREE DEFINING DIFFERENCES

WHILE ALL MANCALA games are alike in general, many variations have developed over time. These variations differ in a number of ways, but among the most notable differences are the type of gameboard used, the method of capturing, and the object of the game. It is these differences that are used to organize mancala games into categories or "versions". An overview of these differences is given here, so that you will have a general means of comparing and contrasting games. Differences will be discussed in more detail in the following chapters on individual games.

DIFFERENT GAMEBOARDS

Most Americans are familiar with the two-row mancala board with six cups per row and a reservoir at each end. However, many other styles of gameboards are also used. All are similar in that they consist of rows of cups through which playing pieces are sown (although there are a few exceptions). However, they differ in detail.

Mancala gameboards can have two, three, or four **rows of cups**. Boards with two rows are by far the most common, being used in most places where mancala is played. Four-row gameboards are the next most common, being used in southern and eastern Africa. The three-row gameboard is the rarest of all. Associated with games of antiquity, it was long thought to be obsolete. However, recent research has turned up several three-row mancala games still played in the mountains of northeastern Africa.

No matter how many rows of cups a mancala board has, it will always have the same number of **cups per row**. However, this number can vary depending on the game. Some boards have as few as three cups per row, presumably meant for children's games. Other boards have as many as twenty-eight cups per row, clearly being intended for advanced players. Such extremes are interesting but rare, however. Most mancala boards have between six and twelve cups per row, the most practical number in terms of constructing the board as well as playing.

Along with the rows of cups, mancala boards, especially two-row boards, often include a large cup at each end called a **reservoir**. Reservoirs are used for storing stones captured during the game. While for many versions that is their only purpose, in most American and Southeast Asian two-row versions, players sow through their own and sometimes both reservoirs just as they would a regular cup. Therefore, reservoirs are always found on boards used for these versions.

While the cups on most mancala gameboards are arranged in rows with a reservoir placed at each end, there is occasionally a gameboard with a different arrangement. For example, the Indian game of Pallanguli sometimes uses a board with cups arranged in a circle with the two reservoirs placed in the middle. Another exception is the board used for Crossroads Mancala, a game for four players created by Happy Viking. It is shaped like an "X" with the cups following its branches in a pattern of right angles. A reservoir is placed at the end of each branch. As different as these gameboards look, though, they are nothing more than traditional boards where the rows have been stretched and bent to accommodate different rules or more players.

METHOD OF CAPTURING

Another major difference among mancala games is the type of capturing used. In general, to capture in mancala, you must land a stone, usually your last stone sown, in a particular cup. Then you are allowed to take the stones held in that or a nearby cup and add them to your winnings. There are many variations of capturing used in mancala. Below are some of the more typical forms. (These forms of capture are explained and illustrated in detail later in this book under the individual version they are associated with.)

One of the most common types of capturing used in mancala is **cross capturing**. In cross capturing, the last stone you sow must land in an empty cup, usually on your side of the board. If there are one or more stones in the adjacent cup on the opposite side of the board, you then capture those stones and usually your last stone sown. This form of capturing is typical of American and Southeast Asian games. It is also used in some African games.

Specific-count capturing is another common form of capturing. In specific-count capturing, the last stone you sow must land in a cup containing a specific number of stones, usually one, two, or three, making the total two, three, or four. You then capture that cup and add the stones to your winnings. This form of capturing is used in mancala games played in Egypt and northern and western Africa as well as the Middle East.

Pull-across capturing is a form of capturing commonly used in African four-row games. In many ways, it is similar to cross capturing. However, there are several important differences. For one thing, in pull-across capturing, your last stone sown must land in a loaded cup on your side of the board rather than an empty cup. In addition, you do not take the stones off the board as you would in cross capturing. Instead, you pull them across to your side of the board and continue sowing them as you would for a regular play.

Skip-cup capturing is an unusual type of capturing in mancala, because what is held in the cup where your last stone lands does not determine if you capture. It is what is held in the cups following it. Specifically, your last stone sown must land in a cup followed by an empty cup that is, in turn, followed by a loaded cup. You then capture the stones held in the third cup. Skip-cup capturing appears mostly in mancala games played in India.

Wegue capturing is a type of capturing in mancala associated with northern African games. **Wegues** themselves are special cups that are created when your last stone sown lands in one of your opponent's cups that originally held three stones. You own any wegues that are established in your cups, and your opponent owns any wegues established in her cups. Players then capture the stones held in the wegues they own by landing their last stone there.

As mentioned before, in most American and Southeast Asian two-row versions, you sow stones through your reservoir as if it were an extra cup. Any stones that land there are yours and stay there for the rest of the game. In most of these games, such **reservoir captures** are a secondary form of capturing that exists in conjunction with a primary form, usually cross capturing. However, there are games where the only means of capturing stones is by landing them in your reservoir.

THE OBJECT OF THE GAME

Single Games

Regarding **single games** (games that are played one time through to determine a winner) there are three types of mancala games as defined by the object of the game. These are capture games, disable games, and go-empty games. In **capture games**, the object is to capture more stones than your opponent by the end of the game. Most two-row versions are capture games.

In **disable games**, the object is to leave your opponent unable to play. You do this by making strategic captures that either clear your opponent's side of the board of all stones or leave her an arrangement of stones she can not play. The number of stones captured is not important. Most four-row games and some two-row games are disable games.

Go-empty games are like disable games, except you do just the reverse. You try to clear your side of the board of stones rather than your opponent's side. Again, the number of stones captured is not important. A few American two-row games are go-empty games.

The object of any mancala game is always one of the three above. However, one of the other two is often strategically tied in. For example, assume you are playing a two-row capture game. The game ends when your side is cleared of stones or **goes empty**, and you keep any stones remaining on your opponent's side. You can use the go-empty ending in your strategy. That is, if your side goes empty at the right time, you can capture enough stones to win the game.

Conversely, assume you are playing a four-row disable game that uses pull-across capture. The object is to clear your opponent's side of the board of stones. Since in four-row games, you sow only through your two rows, the only way you have of clearing your opponent's side is by capturing her stones to your side. In this way, capturing more stones is essential to a winning strategy.

Because objects are often strategically tied, many mancala games can be converted from a capture game to a go-empty or disable game (and vice versa) with minimal changes to the rules. The difference shows up in playing. The strategies needed to win a capture game, a disable game, and a go-empty game are all very different.

Games Played in Rounds

Most Americans play mancala as a single game. However, in many parts of the world mancala is played in **rounds** where several games are played to determine the winner. In such games, also called matches, the object, or **ultimate goal**, may not be the same as the object of any one round.

There are several types of ultimate goals found among mancala matches. One of the simplest involves winning more games of a match than your opponent. The African four-row game of Hus is played this way. Another ultimate goal is keeping a tally of stones captured over the duration of the match. The first to reach a certain score is the winner. The Egyptian two-row game of Mankala'h is played this way.

However, many mancala matches have a more complex ultimate goal. For instance, in the two-row versions of Filipino Sungka and Indian Pallanguli, the ultimate goal is to disable your opponent by putting her cups out of play. This is done by winning and hoarding as many stones as you can from round to round. Any cups you can not fill at the beginning of a new round become inactive. Finally, one player has so few active cups that he can not continue playing.

In other games, like the African two-row versions of Wari and Adi, you capture your opponent's cups over a series of rounds. It is again done by winning and hoarding as many stones as you can from round to round. You capture any cups your opponent can not fill at the beginning of a new round. Your opponent becomes increasingly limited and is ultimately at too much of a disadvantage to continue.

OTHER DIFFERENCES

THERE ARE MANY other differences among mancala games besides the three defining ones discussed above. For instance, how the board is set up or how the game is started and ended varies. Whether a single or continued play is used varies, and so on. While such differences do not define new versions of mancala, they have a definite effect on the game and yield many variations within versions.

Again, only an overview of these differences is given here for comparison purposes. They will be discussed in more detail later in this book in the chapters on individual games.

PLAYING PIECES

In mancala, you do not own the **playing pieces** nor do they have value. So, their size, color, and shape are not important. The number of pieces you need to play, however, varies with the game. Most games require between forty and one hundred pieces. Individual game instructions will indicate the exact number.

You may change the number of playing pieces a game calls for, but it may change the game. In some cases, the effect is only slight. Periodically, though, the mathematics are such that the game becomes unplayable, because one player can clear the board on a single turn. (Note: for simplicity, playing pieces will generally be referred to as "stones" from here on.)

PARTS OF THE GAMEBOARD

As discussed earlier, mancala gameboards almost all consist of two to four rows of cups with a varying but equal number of cups per row. Many boards, especially two-row boards, also have reservoirs for storing captured stones. Despite the variations, though, the basic rules regarding cups and reservoirs are similar among mancala games.

In most mancala games, the **cups** are divided such that you and your opponent each "own" half the cups, usually the half that you face when the board is placed horizontally between you. It is from these cups that you start your plays and execute your strategy. Not all mancala games have cup ownership, however. In a few, you may start a play from any cup on the board. Such games, mostly American, are rare, though, as starting a play from any cup often gives the first player too much of an advantage. However, in games where this is balanced by other rules, non-ownership of cups can add an interesting twist to the strategy.

In all mancala games, cups are either loaded or empty. **Loaded** means they hold at least one stone. **Empty** means they contain no stones at all. Additionally, cups may be active, inactive, or restricted.

An **active cup** is one that is fully in play. There are no restrictions on it, and you may use it to start a play, sow through it, capture it, or make captures from it. Most mancala games start with all cups active. An **inactive cup** is just the opposite. It is a cup that is fully out of play. You may not use it in any way, not even to sow through. Generally, a cup becomes inactive because some criterion has not been met, and it will stay inactive for the entire game. Inactive cups occur most often in games played in rounds. Usually, they can become active again in a later round once the criterion has been met.

Some games have **restricted cups**. That is, you may sow through or capture them, but you may not start a play from them. For example, in many four-row games, you may not start a play from a **singleton**, a cup holding only one stone. In some two-row games, you may not start a play from a cup holding four stones.

In most cases, restricted cups can become active again within the same game. This is usually when the criterion that restricted them no longer exists. For instance, sowing a stone into a restricted singleton makes that cup active again, because it no longer holds just one stone. Similarly, a cup restricted because it holds four stones becomes active again when a fifth stone is sown into it.

Reservoirs are usually present on two-row and three-row mancala boards, but only occasionally on four-row boards. Unlike cups, however, whether they are owned or not depends on the game. For disable and go-empty games where the number of stones captured is not important, players do not own a reservoir. For capture games where players do need to keep track of their captured stones, however, reservoirs are owned.

In capture games where stones are not played through the reservoir, it does not matter which reservoir you own as long as you and your opponent keep your stones separate. Traditionally, players use the reservoir on their right. However, in games where stones are sown through the reservoir, which reservoir you own is important. Typically, it will be the reservoir on your right for a game played in a counterclockwise direction, the left for a clockwise game.

SETTING UP THE GAMEBOARD

Setting up the gameboard refers to arranging the stones prior to playing. In mancala, there are two types of setups, a fixed setup and a strategic setup. In a **fixed setup**, the gameboard is arranged according to a set of rules. Both players begin with the same number and arrangement of stones, theoretically giving them the same starting advantages. A player is then randomly chosen to go first.

In some mancala games, rather than using a fixed setup, one player arranges the stones on the board to suit his strategy. This is called a **strategic setup**. Usually this player has considerable freedom in how he does this. The only restrictions are that he must be sure each player gets half or close to half of the stones. In addition, once the board is set up, his opponent makes the first play.

It may appear that the strategic setup leaves the opponent a victim of whatever she is doled. This is seldom the case, however. In some games if she does not like the setup, she may turn the board around. In others, she is allowed to rearrange her side. In either case, though, she forfeits her right to go first.

DIRECTION OF PLAY

In mancala, the stones are sown repeatedly around the board. This sowing forms a circular pattern and plays are said to be made in a **clockwise** or **counterclockwise direction**. While the majority of games are counterclockwise, in some you sow clockwise. This may seem significant, but it is not. The direction of play in mancala does not matter as long as you are consistent (a rare instance where a change does not affect mancala). Therefore, you may change directions if you like. However, keep in mind that for games where you sow through your reservoir, you must also switch reservoirs. Otherwise, you will find yourself playing a very different game.

Most mancala games are played in only one direction, but there are exceptions. In some two-row games, for instance, you choose your direction of play before beginning the game. This may result in you and your opponent playing in opposite directions. In other two-row games, the direction you sow depends on the cup from which you started your play. In addition, in some four-row games, you may reverse your direction of sowing if you can make a capture.

While they are rare, a few games allow you to sow in any direction you like, even changing directions during the same turn. However, if there are no compensating rules, such games tend to be too trivial to be interesting.

TYPES OF PLAYS

To make a play in mancala, you pick up all the stones from any one of your cups and sow them around the board. There are variations on how and when this is done, however, resulting in different types of plays.

The **single play** is the simplest play of all in mancala, because you pick up and sow only one cup of stones. It does not matter what is held in the cup where your last stone lands. Once you finish sowing, your turn ends. Games with single play occur most often in western African and some American variations.

Continued play is the most commonly used play in mancala, occurring in games worldwide. It starts like a single play in that you pick up and sow the stones from any one of your cups. However, your turn does not necessarily end once you sow that last stone. If this stone lands in a loaded cup, you continue by picking up those stones and sowing them as you did before, starting with the next cup. You do this until your last stone sown lands in an empty cup or your reservoir in games where you sow through the reservoir.

There is one drawback to continued play. A few games exist where the right combination of moves can result in one player winning before the second has a chance to play. If you are playing a game and this occurs, try changing the setup so you start with three or five stones per cup, for example, instead of four. You may also establish a rule that neither player may use the particular play that originally caused the problem.

Continued play has several variations. One of these is **limited continued play** where continued play is restricted to one side of the board. There are two variations of this. In one, if your last stone sown lands in a loaded cup on your side, you may make a continued play. If it lands in a loaded cup on your opponent's side, your turn ends even if your last play was a continued play. The opposite situation also occurs. Limited continued play is seldom found in mancala and is mainly a characteristic of a few American variations.

Another form of continued play is **next-cup continued play**. In next-cup continued play you ignore the cup where your last stone lands. Instead, you continue sowing if your last stone sown lands in a cup followed by a loaded cup. You take the stones from the second cup and sow them starting with the cup following that one.

Next-cup continued play is mainly associated with Indian Pallanguli, but it occasionally appears in a few American games. An interesting twist is that in American games the next cup sometimes includes your reservoir. Thus, if your last stone sown lands in your rightmost cup, you must sow the entire contents of your reservoir back onto the board.

A **simultaneous play** is a continued play where you and your opponent sow your stones at the same time, sowing until you have each landed your last stone in an empty cup. Traditionally, this play is only used once at the beginning of a game to randomize the board so the first player will not have too much of an advantage. However, we have encountered a few American players who play simultaneously throughout the game! As far as we can tell, the simultaneous play appears sporadically in mancala. The games known to use it include certain Southeast Asian games such as Filipino Sungka and a few African games.

A **go-again play** is different from the plays discussed above in that it is essentially another turn. There are two types of go-again plays. One is the **capture go-again play**. In essence, if you make a capture, you get another turn. This play is found in many Egyptian and Indian versions. A second type of go-again play is the **reservoir go-again play**. It only occurs in games where you sow through one or both reservoirs. In this play, any time your last stone sown lands in your reservoir (or in some variations your opponent's reservoir) you get another turn.

SECONDARY CAPTURING

The primary types of capturing used in mancala, the types that define different versions, have already been discussed in the last chapter. However, in many mancala games a secondary type of capturing is allowed. It never replaces the primary type but does provide a means of picking up some extra stones. There are many types of secondary capturing. Below are some of the more common ones.

In some mancala games, such as those played in India and parts of Africa, players may capture cups we call **passing-fours**. A passing-four is formed when a player sows a stone other than his last into a cup that held three stones and makes its total four. Passing-fours are available for capture as they form. However, who may capture them depends on the game.

Frequently in mancala, you may take the stones from an extra cup when you capture. This is called **bonus-cup capturing**, and it is most characteristic of African versions. Generally, the bonus cup must be adjacent to the one you captured, although there are exceptions. In addition, specific games may add further restrictions to keep bonus capturing from getting out of hand. While most games with bonus-cup capturing allow taking the stones from only one bonus cup, a few allow you to take stones from a second or even third one. These additional cups must usually be next to your first bonus cup but sometimes they may be cups of your own choosing.

Similar to bonus-cup capturing is **series capturing**, most often associated with African Wari and Egyptian Mankala'h. Series capturing is best explained using the example of Wari. In Wari, you capture by landing your last stone sown in a cup on your opponent's side of the board that originally held one or two stones, making its total two or three. If the preceding cup and any consecutive cups before it also hold two or three stones and are on your opponent's side, you capture those stones as well. Series capturing works similarly in Egyptian Mankala'h, except you are not limited to your opponent's side only.

Most variations of Wari limit series capturing, not allowing you to take the stones from the last cup in the series if it would clear your opponent's side. However, in some variations, especially those played in the United States, you are allowed to capture the stones from all six cups on your opponent's side. This is called **grand capturing**, and it is a powerful play. It is also one of the most difficult plays to make in mancala.

Alternating cup capturing occurs in some variations of Pallanguli. It is like series capturing in general, but the specifics are different. In Pallanguli you capture by landing your last stone sown in a cup followed by an empty cup that is in turn is followed by a loaded cup. You then take the stones held in the third cup. If the third cup is followed by an empty cup that is in turn followed by a loaded cup, you additionally take the stones held in the fifth cup. You continue in this manner until the alternating pattern is interrupted.

Because it is a tempting jackpot, it is not surprising that American Cross Capture variations have developed where you can capture your opponent's reservoir. This is called **reservoir capturing**. (We also refer to it as a **nasty capture**.) These games still rely on cross capturing as the primary form of capture. However, by making the right play, you can additionally capture the stones held in your opponent's reservoir.

ENDING THE GAME

Although the specifics vary with the game, all mancala games end when one of three situations occurs:

- You make a play and all of the cups on your side of the board become empty
- It is your opponent's turn and she can no longer play because
    You made a play that cleared her side or left her stones but none she can play
        or
    She made a play that left her no future plays, and you cannot play anything to
        her on your next turn
- The entire board is cleared of stones, and neither player has stones in his/her cups

Once the game ends, who wins depends on the type of game being played. In capture games, the winner is the player to capture more stones. It does not matter how the game ends. However, for go-empty and disable games, the way the game ends determines the winner. The number of stones captured is unimportant.

Occasionally in mancala, situations occur where the game has not ended but no more meaningful plays are possible. This is known as a **stalemate**, and it occurs most often in games that use specific-count capturing with a clear-the-entire-board ending. In such games, players usually decide on rules for handling stalemates at the beginning of the game.

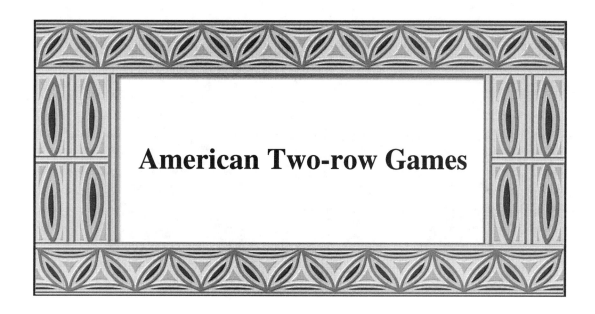

American Two-row Games

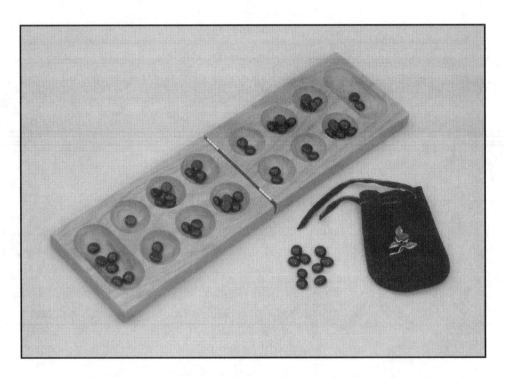

Folding American mancala board made by authors.

SIMPLE CAPTURE MANCALA

IN TERMS OF rules, Simple Capture Mancala is probably the easiest version of mancala you can play, mainly because there is no particular type of capture. The only way you gain stones is by landing them in your reservoir as you sow, although some variations allow a secondary form of capture.

In regard to history, it is not known exactly how Simple Capture Mancala developed. However, it appears to be a simplification of the American favorite, Cross Capture Mancala, discussed in the next chapter. The two versions are nearly the same, except in Simple Capture Mancala, cross capturing has been dropped.

Several Simple Capture Mancala games are included in this chapter, many with variations of their own. These games fall into two groups: capture games and go-empty games.

CAPTURE GAMES

SIMPLE CAPTURE MANCALA 1
The Basic Game

Simple Capture Mancala 1 is the easiest of the easiest mancala games you can play. Not only are its rules very basic, but it requires almost no strategy to win. For this reason, it is ideal for young children. This game has several variations that follow the basic instructions. By adding one or more, the game becomes more interesting for adults.

Object: To capture more stones than your opponent by the end of the game.

Gameboard: The gameboard consists of two rows of six cups and a reservoir at each end for storing stones captured during the game. Each player owns the row of six cups nearest him. Thus, your cups would be cups "A" through "F" and your opponent's cups, "a" through "f", as shown below. Reservoirs are also owned. Players each own the reservoir on their right.

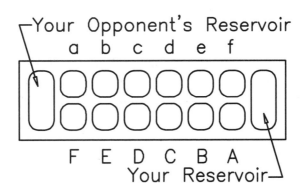

Board Setup: Forty-eight stones are required. Place four stones in each of the twelve cups, leaving the two reservoirs empty.

Playing:

Randomly choose a player to start. To make a play, take all the stones from any one of your six cups and sow them all counterclockwise around the board. Sow one stone per cup, starting with the cup next to the one from which you originally took the stones. Sow through all twelve cups plus your reservoir but not your opponent's reservoir. All stones that land in your reservoir are yours and remain there until the end of the game. The following figures illustrate this play, called a single play.

Assume that the game is in progress and you choose to move the stones from cup "D". Before you start your play, the board looks like this.

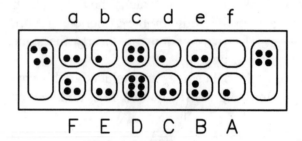

You pick up all six stones from cup "D", and leaving "D" empty, sow one stone each into cups "C", "B", and "A". You then sow a stone into your reservoir and continue onto your opponent's side, dropping a stone into cup "f" and your last stone into cup "e". The play then ends, and the board looks like this.

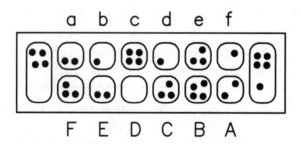

For a single play, once you finish sowing, your play ends. However, if your last stone sown lands in your reservoir, you get another turn. Take the stones from any cup on your side of the board and sow them counterclockwise around the board as you did before. This is called a reservoir go-again play. Otherwise, your opponent makes the next play.

Ending:

The game ends when you complete a play and all six cups on your side of the board go empty. You capture all the stones remaining in your opponent's cups but not her reservoir. Move the captured stones to your reservoir. The player who has captured more stones wins.

Variations:

Add last stone capture

Play as directed above, except if the last stone you sow lands in an empty cup on your side of the board, you capture that stone. Place the captured stone in your reservoir. Your opponent makes the next play.

Add continued play

Play as described for a single play, except if the last stone you sow lands in a cup on either side of the board that already contains one or more stones, continue playing. Take the stones from that cup and sow them around the board as before, starting with the next cup. Continue sowing in this manner until the last stone you sow lands in your reservoir or an empty cup. The next set of figures illustrates the continued play.

Assume that the game is in progress, and you choose to start your next play from cup "F". Before you make your play, the board looks like this.

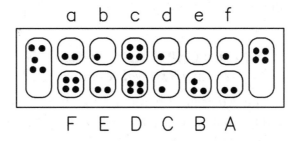

Your last stone sown lands in cup "B", which contains several stones and the board now looks like this.

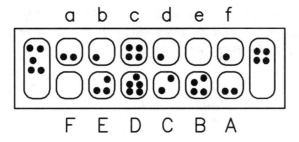

You then pick up the stones in cup "B" including your last stone sown, and leaving "B" empty, sow them in the same direction, starting with cup "A". The stones on the board are now arranged like this.

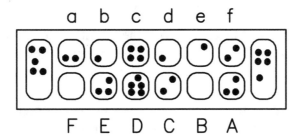

As shown above, the last of the stones sown landed in cup "e", which was previously empty. Therefore, the continued play ended.

27

SIMPLE CAPTURE MANCALA 2
Start a Play from Any Cup

Play as directed under Simple Capture Mancala 1 discussed above, except for the following changes. First, you may start a play from either side of the board, not just one of your six cups. Second, the game ends when both sides of the board are empty of all stones. Once the entire board is cleared, the player with more captured stones wins. You may add any of the variations from Simple Capture Mancala 1 to this game.

Notes on Strategy:

There is only a slight change of rules from Simple Capture Mancala 1, but it results in a game with much more strategy. In Simple Capture Mancala 2, you have twice as many options when starting a play. However, you no longer control one side of the board, so setting up plays is more difficult. The trick is to get the majority of stones to your side. This will slow your opponent down. Do not rely on taking those stones by forcing your opponent to go empty, though, since the game does not end until the entire board is empty.

SIMPLE CAPTURE MANCALA 3
Passive Reservoir Capture

Play like Simple Capture Mancala 1 with the variation continued play, except for the following changes. First, continued play is limited to your side of the board only. This means if the last stone you sow lands in a loaded cup on your side of the board, you continue playing. Take the stones from that cup and sow them as you normally would, starting with the next cup. However, if the last stone you sow lands in a loaded cup on your opponent's side of the board, your turn ends.

Finally, if your last stone sown lands in an empty cup on your side of the board, your turn ends as it normally would. However, if it lands in an empty cup on your opponent's side of the board, she captures all the stones in your reservoir, called a passive reservoir capture. Your turn then ends, and your opponent makes the next play.

Notes on Strategy:

The unique feature of this variation is that your opponent can passively capture your reservoir. At the beginning of the game when there are many stones on the board, you can avoid this. However, as the stones thin out, it will be more difficult. You will need to plan carefully to avoid sowing to your opponent's side.

SIMPLE CAPTURE MANCALA 4
Deadstone Mancala

Play like Simple Capture Mancala 1 with the variation continued play, except do not sow beyond your opponent's rightmost cup "a" (next to her reservoir) even on a continued play. If you reach this cup and have stones left over, your turn ends, but you may be able to capture the leftover stones.

To capture, there may be any number of stones in your opponent's rightmost cup, but your leftmost cup (cup "F" across from her rightmost cup) must be empty. If this is the case, take the leftover stones, leaving the one you sowed into her rightmost cup, and place them in your reservoir. Your opponent makes the next play. Otherwise, the leftover stones become **deadstones** and are permanently removed from the board, never counting among either player's winnings.

Variations:

Add jackpot capture

At Happy Viking, we have developed a variation of this game. Play as described above, except for the following change. Deadstones that are not immediately captured are stored in a separate jackpot (not in either reservoir). Either player may capture the jackpot at any time during the game. To do this, you must reach your opponent's rightmost cup and your leftmost cup must be empty, just as before. You then capture the jackpot plus any stones you were unable to sow. Take your captured stones and place them in your reservoir. Your opponent makes the next play. After the game has ended, any deadstones remaining in the jackpot are not counted among either player's winnings.

GO-EMPTY GAMES

SIMPLE CAPTURE MANCALA 5
Go-empty 1

Go-empty 1 is played like Simple Capture Mancala 1 with the variation continued play. However, in Go-empty 1, the object is not to capture more stones. Instead, it is to clear your side of the board of stones before your opponent. The number of stones you capture by the end of the game will not matter. Other than this, there are no differences between this game and Simple Capture Mancala 1.

Notes on Strategy:

This is a small change concerning the rules, but it takes an entirely different strategy to win the game. No longer will capturing more stones be your main intent. In fact, focusing too much on this can actually hurt your strategy. Instead, you will want to focus on shifting the stones to your opponent's side. Capturing stones will only be used to help you achieve that goal.

SIMPLE CAPTURE MANCALA 6
Go-empty 2

Go-empty 2 is played like Simple Capture Mancala 1 with single play except for the following changes. First, start the game with three stones per cup instead of four. Second, you may sow either clockwise or counterclockwise on any turn. However, you may not change directions during a turn. Third, sow through both reservoirs, not just your own. Since this game has reservoir go-again, if your last stone sown lands in either reservoir, take another turn.

Variations:

Move the stones to another cup in place of your regular turn

This substitute play is useful in setting up future plays. Instead of sowing them, place all the stones from any one of your cups into an adjacent cup. The adjacent cup may be on either side of the original cup but must be on your side of the board and may not be a reservoir. Do not sow the stones farther. Your turn ends and your opponent makes the next play.

Add continued play

This game did not originally have continued play, but we found that it made it more interesting. To add continued play, follow the instructions under variations for Simple Capture Mancala 1. However, increase the numbers of stones you start the game with to four per cup. Otherwise, the mathematics work out such that the first player can clear the board on his first turn.

**American mancala board made of layered hardwoods from
authors' collection.**

CROSS CAPTURE MANCALA

CROSS CAPTURE MANCALA is probably the most popular version of mancala played in the United States. It is played similarly to Simple Capture Mancala, except that it adds cross capturing. When or where Cross Capture Mancala got its start, though, is difficult to say. As discussed previously, mancala games, specifically Wari, arrived in the United States with the first Africans. In the late 1800s, a Syrian version Chuba was introduced that popularized mancala with Americans in general. However, Wari and Chuba are played very differently from Cross Capture Mancala. They use specific-count capturing and no plays are made through the reservoirs.

After doing some research, however, we found some interesting coincidences that may shed light on the origins of Cross Capture Mancala. The rules for this version are very similar to a version played in Southeast Asia called Sungka. In Sungka, you sow through your reservoir and cross capturing is used. The only differences are that Sungka is played on a board with seven cups per row instead of six. In addition, it is played in rounds.

It is possible that Cross Capture Mancala is a descendant of Sungka, either directly such as being introduced by immigrants or indirectly through a commercial game like the 1950s game *Kalah* (which has Cross Capture rules). Playing in rounds was dropped and the game adapted to the shorter, more convenient gameboard used for Wari and Chuba.

Cross Capture Mancala has numerous variations. For instance, there are games where you can cross capture from your side of the board only, your opponent's side only, or both sides of the board. The variations, in turn, have variations of their own such as different ways to start and end the game. Included in this chapter are some of the more interesting Cross Capture games we have encountered. They are divided into two sections: basic capture games and more challenging capture games where you can capture your opponent's reservoir or lose your own.

Unlike Simple Capture Mancala, we have encountered few go-empty or disable Cross Capture games. Therefore, they have no separate section. However, instructions are included for converting capture games at the end of this chapter.

BASIC CAPTURE GAMES

CROSS CAPTURE MANCALA 1
The Basic Game: Cross Capture from Your Side Only

Cross Capture Mancala 1 with cross capture from your side only is the best known Cross Capture game there is. Ask any American mancala player how they play, and this will almost invariably be the game they show you. Among commercial manufacturers, Cross Capture Mancala 1 has become a standard.

Cross Capture Mancala 1 has numerous variations. Some of the more interesting ones are included below. Learn the basic game first, and then try it with a variation or two. You may be surprised at how differently the game plays. Unless stated otherwise, any number or combination of variations may be used.

Object: To capture more stones than your opponent by the end of the game.

Gameboard: The gameboard consists of two rows of six cups and a reservoir at each end for storing stones captured during the game. Each player owns the row of six cups nearest him. Thus, your cups would be cups "A" through "F" and your opponent's cups, "a" through "f", as shown below. Reservoirs are also owned. Players each own the reservoir on their right.

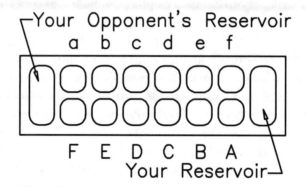

Board Setup: Forty-eight stones are required. Place four stones in each of the twelve cups, leaving the two reservoirs empty.

Playing:

Randomly choose a player to start. To make a play, take the stones from any one cup on your side of the board. Sow them all counterclockwise around the board, one per cup, leaving the cup you originally took the stones from empty. You may sow through all twelve cups plus your reservoir but not your opponent's reservoir. This play, called a single play, is shown in the figures below.

Assume that the game is in progress and you choose to move the stones from cup "D". Before you start your play, the board looks like this.

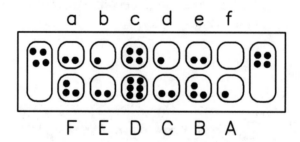

You pick up all six stones from cup "D", and leaving "D" empty, sow one stone each into cups "C", "B", and "A". You continue by sowing a stone into your reservoir and onto your opponent's side, dropping a stone into cup "f" and your last stone into cup "e". The play then ends, and the board looks like this.

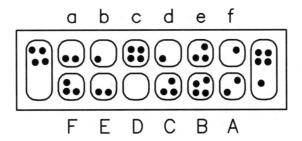

For a single play, once you finish sowing, your play ends. However, if your last stone sown lands in your reservoir, you get another turn. Take the stones from any cup on your side of the board and sow them counterclockwise around the board as you did before. This is called a reservoir go-again play.

If the last stone you sow lands in an empty cup, your turn also ends, but you may be able to cross capture. If the empty cup is on your side of the board and there are one or more stones in the adjacent cup on your opponent's side of the board, then you capture those stones plus your last stone sown. Place them in your reservoir. Your opponent makes the next play. Cross capturing is illustrated by the following figures.

Assume the game is in progress. You see that if you start your next play from cup "E, you can capture the stones held in your opponent's cup "e". Before you make your play, the board looks like this.

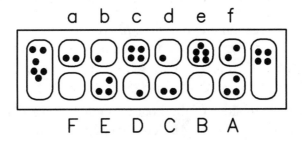

You pick up the stones from cup "E", and leaving it empty sow them one by one into the adjacent cups. Your last stone sown lands in cup "B", which was previously empty. Since cup "B" is across from cup "e" on your opponent's side and cup "e" contains several stones, you make a capture. Take the stones from your opponent's cup plus your last stone sown and place them in your reservoir.

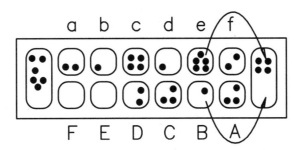

After you take the stones, the board looks like this.

35

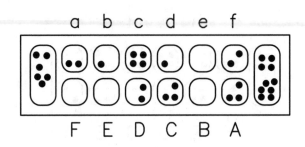

Ending:

Ending 1: Clear your side

This is the ending, also called a go-empty ending, most typically used with this game. The game ends when you make a play and all six cups on your side of the board become empty. You capture all the stones remaining in your opponent's cups. Move these stones to your reservoir. The winner is the player who has more stones in his reservoir.

Ending 2: Clear your opponent's side

The game ends when it is your opponent's turn and she can no longer play because:

- You made a play that cleared her side
- She made a play that cleared her side and you can play nothing to her on your next turn

You capture all the stones that remain on your side. Move them to your reservoir. However, if your opponent makes a play that clears her side, and you can play something to her on your next turn, the game continues.

Ending 3: Clear the entire board

The game ends when both sides of the board go empty. The player who has more captured stones wins. If one player's side goes empty before this happens, he passes until his opponent plays something to his side. The opponent must do so as soon as she can.

Variations:

Add continued play

Play as described above, except for the following change. If the last stone you sow lands in a loaded cup on either side of the board, continue playing. Take the stones from that cup and sow them around the board as before, starting with the next cup. Continue sowing in this manner until the last stone you sow lands in your reservoir or an empty cup. The following set of figures illustrates the continued play.

Assume that the game is in progress, and you choose to start your next play from cup "F". Before you make your play, the board looks like this.

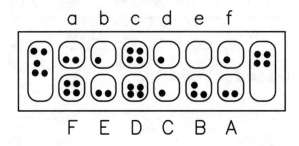

Your last stone sown lands in cup "B", which contains several stones and the board now looks like this.

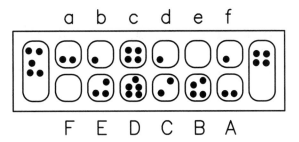

You then pick up the stones in cup "B", including your last stone sown, and leaving "B" empty, sow them in the same direction, starting with cup "A". The stones on the board are now arranged like this.

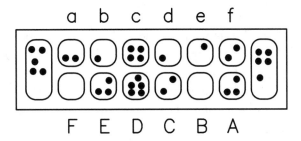

As seen in the figure above, the last of the stones sown landed in cup "e", which was previously empty. Therefore, the continued play ended.

Add last-stone capture

Play as you normally would, except if the last stone you sow lands in an empty cup on your side of the board, you capture that stone even if you are unable to make a cross capture. Place the captured stone in your reservoir. Your turn ends and your opponent makes the next play.

Play through both reservoirs

Play as you normally would, except sow through both reservoirs instead of just your own. This means you will be building your opponent's reservoir as well as your own.

This variation works best with single play as described in the basic instructions. In the case of continued play, it is all too easy to fill your opponent's reservoir, especially toward the beginning of the game. If you choose to use continued play anyway, a good strategy is trying to make plays where you end before reaching your opponent's reservoir. In addition, you may want to rely more heavily on cross capture to gain stones than sowing through your reservoir.

CROSS CAPTURE MANCALA 2
Limited Continued Play, Your Side Only

Cross Capture Mancala 2 is played like Cross Capture Mancala 1 with the variation continued play, except continued play is limited to your side of the board only. Thus, if the last stone you sow lands in a loaded cup on your side of the board, continue playing. However, if it lands in a loaded cup on your opponent's side of the board, your turn ends.

Any ending used for Cross Capture Mancala 1 will work with this game, although Ending 2, clearing your opponent's side, works best. This ending is also the best one to use if you convert this game to a disable game, as discussed at the end of this chapter. In addition, any of the other variations for Cross Capture Mancala 1 may be added to this game.

Notes on Strategy:

Limited continued play does not initially affect the game. However, when there are only a few stones left on the board, you will notice a difference. This is because limited continued play often forces you to play to your opponent's side and then end there. This is contrary to your goal of trying to force your opponent to go empty so you can end the game and keep what remains on your side. Interestingly, this combination is what lends this game so well to conversion to a disable game (explained later).

CROSS CAPTURE MANCALA 3
Limited Continued Play, Your Opponent's Side Only

Cross Capture Mancala 3 is played like Cross Capture Mancala 1 with the variation continued play, except continued play is limited to your opponent's side of the board only. This means, if the last stone you sow lands in a loaded cup on your opponent's side of the board, you continue playing. If it lands in a loaded cup on your side of the board, your turn ends.

Any ending used for Cross Capture Mancala 1 will work for this game, although Ending 1, you go empty, works best. This ending is also the best one to use if you convert this game to a go-empty game, as discussed at the end of this chapter. In addition, any of the variations for Cross Capture Mancala 1 may be added to this game.

Notes on Strategy:

Regarding rules, this game is a mirror image of the previous one. However, the challenges must be approached from the opposite angle. The result is that a different strategy is required to win, making the two variations play quite differently.

CROSS CAPTURE MANCALA 4
Cross Capture from Your Opponent's Side Only

Cross Capture Mancala 4 is played like Cross Capture Mancala 1, except that you cross capture from your opponent's side of the board rather than your own. This means that only when the last stone you sow lands in an empty cup on your opponent's side of the board, and there are one or more stones in the adjacent cup on your side, you capture. Take your captured stones plus your last stone sown and place them in your reservoir. Your opponent makes the next play. The **opposite-side cross capture** is shown below.

Assume the game is in progress. You see that if you start your next play from cup "A", you can capture the stones held in your cup "C". Before you make your play, the board looks like this.

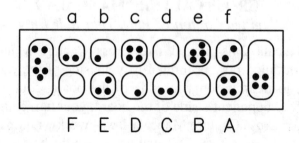

You pick up the stones from cup "A", and leaving it empty, sow them one by one into your reservoir, then cups "f" and "e". As shown below, your last stone sown lands in cup "d", which was previously empty.

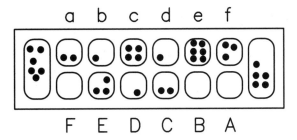

Since cup "d" is across from cup "C" on your side and contains several stones, you make a capture. Take the stones from cup "C" plus your last stone sown and place them in your reservoir. After you take the stones, the board looks like this.

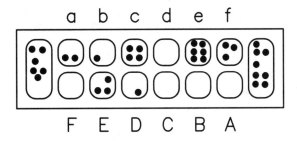

Any ending described under Cross Capture Mancala 1 may be used with this game, although Ending 1, you go empty, is the one most typically used. In addition, any of the other variations for Cross Capture Mancala 1 may be added to this game.

Notes on Strategy:

Although cross capturing from your opponent's side is only a slight modification to the rules, it affects the strategy considerably. This is because your opponent, rather than you, has control of the cups from which you are trying to cross capture. Further, while you are trying to set up your side of the board to make a cross capture, you must simultaneously defend it from your opponent.

CROSS CAPTURE MANCALA 5
Cross Capture from Either Side of the Board

Cross Capture Mancala 5 is the next logical step in basic Cross Capture games. It is played like Cross Capture Mancala 1 with single play, except you can cross capture from either side of the board. This means if your last stone sown lands in an empty cup anywhere on the board, and the adjacent cup on the other side is loaded, you capture those stones. Take them plus your last stone sown, and place them in your reservoir. Your opponent makes the next play. (See Cross Capture Mancala 1 and Cross Capture Mancala 4 for illustrations of this.)

Cross Capture Mancala 5 may be played with any ending listed under Cross Capture Mancala 1, although Ending 3, clearing the board, works best. The variations, though, do not work well. With cross capture from both sides, this game already plays fast. Since these variations would speed the game up even more (by adding more ways to take stones off the board), the game would become pointless. However, Cross Capture Mancala 5 has some interesting variations of its own that are included below.

Variations:

Start a play from either side

Play as directed above, except when starting a play you may take the stones from any one cup (never a reservoir) on either side of the board rather than just your cups.

Choose your direction of play

Play as directed, except that once both players have had a first turn, you may choose your direction of play. This means you may sow clockwise or counterclockwise on any turn. However, you may never reverse the direction of sowing during any one turn.

Notes on Strategy:

Allowing cross capturing from either side of the board makes this game play faster than other Cross Capture games. Early in the game, players will be racing to make cross captures when they are easiest to make. Reservoir go-again plays will be secondary to cross capturing. Later, when there are fewer stones left on the board, the game slows down.

CROSS CAPTURE MANCALA 6
Cross Capture from Either Side of the Board, Add Rams

Cross Capture Mancala 6 is played like Cross Capture Mancala 5 where you cross capture from either side of the board, but it adds **rams**. Rams are restricted cups that sometimes occur in single play games. (They do not work in continued play games.) You may not start a play from a ram, although you may sow through one, building its contents. Rams may also be cross captured.

Your cups become rams when they contain enough stones to sow around the board and back onto your side. Thus, the number of stones needed to make a ram varies from cup to cup. For instance, if your leftmost cup, cup "F", holds twelve stones and a thirteenth stone is sown into it (by either player and not necessarily the last stone sown), it becomes a ram. If your rightmost cup, cup "A", holds seven stones and an eighth stone is sown into it, it also becomes a ram. Again, this is because if you were to pick up either cup and sow its contents, you would return to your side of the board.

Once a cup becomes a ram, it remains so for the rest of the game unless it is captured, in which case it reverts to an active cup. This means as you play, the number of stones held in any rams will increase.

To make a play, take all the stones from any one of your six cups that are not rams, and sow them all counterclockwise around the board. Sow one stone per cup, starting with the cup next to the one from which you originally took the stones. You may sow through any cup, including rams, plus your reservoir but never your opponent's reservoir. Because of rams, however, (and the fact that this game is single play) you will never sow back onto your side. If any cup holds enough stones to do this, it becomes a ram.

From here, play as you would for Cross Capture Mancala 5. (Do not use any of its variations, however. They won't work for this game.) However, end the game when one player's side of the board goes empty or she is unable to play because she has nothing remaining but rams. Take any stones remaining on your side and place them in your reservoir, except those held in rams.

Stones held in rams can not be counted among either player's winnings. The player who has captured more stones wins.

Notes on Strategy:

Because you can not start a play from a ram, rams appear to be something to be avoided. However, if you play your strategy right, rams can be an excellent way to make a substantial capture. Rams may be cross captured at any time during the game, and you may capture your opponent's rams as well as your own. The only danger is if a ram is ever threatened, it can not be played.

CROSS CAPTURE MANCALA 7
Pull-across Capture

Cross Capture Mancala 7 is played similarly to Cross Capture Mancala 1 with the variation continued play. The difference is that when you cross capture, the stones are not removed from the board and placed in your reservoir. Instead, you "pull" them across to your side of the board, and place them in the cup where your last stone landed. This is similar to the pull-across capture typically used in African four-row games and is illustrated below.

Assume the game is in progress. You see that if you start your next play from cup "E", you can pull across the stones held in cup "e". Before you make your play, the board looks like this.

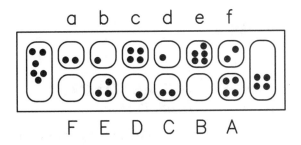

You pick up the stones from cup "E", and leaving it empty, sow them one by one into the following cups. Your last stone sown lands in cup "B".

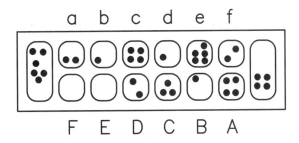

Since cup "B" was previously empty and is across from loaded cup "e", on your opponent's side, you make a capture. Take the stones from "e", but do not remove them from the board. Instead, place them in cup "B". After you place the stones, the board looks like this. Your opponent makes the next play.

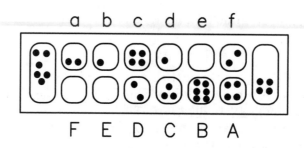

The game ends using Ending 2 described under Cross Capture Mancala 1, when it is your opponent's turn and she can no longer play because her side of the board is empty. You capture the stones remaining on your side.

Notes on Strategy:

The pull-across modification to cross capture adds an interesting twist to the typical cross capture game. This is because it makes clearing your opponent's side of the board as important as capturing more stones. In fact, this game would be a disable game if it were not for the fact that you still capture stones by sowing them into your reservoir.

To win, use pull-across capture to get as many stones to your side as you can. In this way, you can feed them into your reservoir. In addition, this will help you force your opponent to go empty. The earlier in the game you can do this, the more stones you will capture.

LOSE YOUR RESERVOIR GAMES

CROSS CAPTURE MANCALA 8
Death Pocket

Cross Capture Mancala 8 is a combination of Cross Capture Mancala 1 with continued play and an Indian version called Pallanguli. That is, you sow through your reservoir and cross capture just as you would in Cross Capture Mancala 1. However, continued play is done in the style of Pallanguli, which uses next-cup continued play.

In addition, your reservoir is treated like a regular cup on a continued play. This means, if you land your last stone in your rightmost cup and can not make a cross capture, you must pick up and sow all of the stones held in your reservoir.

Start your play as you would in Cross Capture Mancala 1. If the last stone you sow lands in your reservoir, make another play. Take all the stones from any one cup on your side of the board and sow them as described above. If your last stone sown lands in an empty cup on your side of the board, and the adjacent cup on your opponent's side is loaded, take those stones plus your last stone sown and place them in your reservoir. Your turn then ends and your opponent makes the next play.

In all other cases, except one that will be discussed below, if the last stone you sow lands in a cup followed by a loaded cup, continue playing. However, do not take any stones from the cup where your last stone landed. Instead, take the stones from the cup following it, and leaving it empty, sow them as you did before, starting with the cup following the one from which you just took the stones. Continue sowing in this manner until the last stone you sow lands in:

- Your reservoir
- A cup followed by an empty cup

- A cup from which you make a capture
- Your rightmost cup

The following set of figures illustrates the next-cup continued play.

Assume that the game is in progress, and you choose to start your next play from cup "F". Before you make your play, the board looks like this.

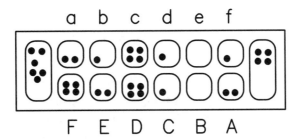

Your last stone sown lands in cup "B". The board now looks like this.

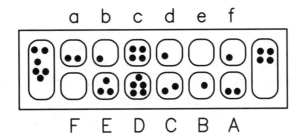

Since cup "e" across from "B" is empty, you can not cross capture. However, since cup "A" following it is loaded, you can continue playing. Pick up the stones in "A" and sow them in the same direction, starting with your reservoir. The stones on the board are now arranged like this.

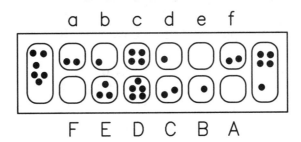

Since your last stone sown landed in cup "f" and cup "e" following it is empty, the continued play ends.

In this game, next-cup continued play also includes your reservoir. Therefore, if your last stone sown lands in your rightmost cup and you can not cross capture, you must sow your reservoir. Remove all of the stones and sow them back onto the board, starting with your opponent's leftmost cup. This is the **death pocket play** alluded to in the title. Continue sowing until one of the aforementioned criteria ends your turn. Your opponent makes the next play.

The game ends using Ending 1 of Cross Capture Mancala 1, you complete a play and all six cups on your side of the board go empty. You capture any stones remaining in your opponent's cups.

Variations:

Play through both reservoirs

Play as you normally would, except sow through both reservoirs instead of just your own. If your last stone sown lands in your opponent's rightmost cup, sow her reservoir. Remove all of the stones and sow them back onto the board, starting with your leftmost cup. (Since there is not cross capture from your opponent's side, there is no capture restriction on this play.)

CROSS CAPTURE MANCALA 9
Nasty Capture – Capture Your Opponent's Reservoir

Cross Capture Mancala 9 is played like Cross Capture Mancala 1 with the variation continued play, except for the following differences. First, you sow through all twelve cups plus both reservoirs. This means you will be feeding stones to your opponent. However, if your last stone sown lands in your opponent's reservoir, you capture all of the stones held there. Take them and place them in your reservoir. Your opponent makes the next play. The game ends when you complete a play and all six cups on your side of the board go empty, Ending 1 under Cross Capture Mancala 1.

Notes on Strategy:

Capturing your opponent's reservoir has a considerable effect on the strategy, making this variation one of most competitive Cross Capture games there is. A lot of the emphasis is on building your reservoir quickly and going empty as soon as you have enough stones to win. This will be difficult, though, as there is continued play, making guarding your reservoir more difficult. In fact, this game has been known to go back and forth several times before a winner finally emerges.

GO-EMPTY AND DISABLE GAMES

With some exceptions, most of the games above can be converted to go-empty or disable games. The only restrictions are that they must have a go-empty or disable ending. Games where the entire board is cleared are not appropriate for conversion. In addition, an ending appropriate to the object to which you are converting should be used.

To convert a game, you change only the object of the game. All other rules stay the same. Thus, if you convert to a go-empty game, the object will become to clear your side of the board of stones before your opponent. Likewise, for a disable game the object will become to clear your opponent's side of the board of stones before she clears yours. In both cases, the number of stones captured by the end of the game will not matter.

Some of the games above are particularly suited for conversion. These are games where there is considerable challenge in ending the game. Cross Capture Mancala 2, Cross Capture Mancala 6, and Cross Capture Mancala 7 are good choices for disable games. Cross Capture Mancala 3 is a good choice for a go-empty game. In fact, some players like these games better when played with a non-capture object.

Changing from a capture game to one of the other two may have little effect on the rules, but it has a significant impact on the strategy. This is because the number of stones captured by each player is no longer important. Instead, you will be concentrating on getting stones off one side. This means you must sometimes pass up captures and go-again plays to avoid working against yourself.

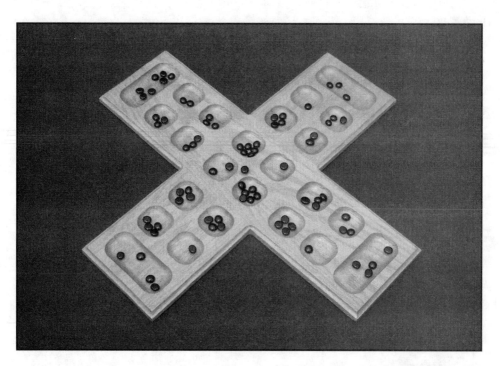

Crossroads board for four players made by authors.

CROSSROADS MANCALA

FOR YEARS, PEOPLE have asked us at Happy Viking if there is a Cross Capture game for four players. There are a few four-player Wari and Adi games. However, we have never encountered a cross capture game for four. That is why we developed Crossroads Mancala.

Crossroads Mancala is similar to Cross Capture Mancala. It is a capture game where you sow through your reservoir, keeping any stones that land there. In addition, it uses cross capturing. Where Crossroads is different is that the board is shaped like a large "X" rather than a rectangle in order to accommodate the extra players. Cups are arranged so they follow the branches of the "X" in a pattern of right angles. (We also developed a variation for three players that uses a "Y" shaped board.)

Two variations of Crossroads are included in this chapter. The first is Basic Crossroads. The rules of this game are straightforward, allowing you to get accustomed to the X-board. Nasty Capture Crossroads follows. It is more aggressive than the basic game, because you can capture your opponents' reservoirs.

CROSSROADS MANCALA 1
The Basic Game

If you have played Cross Capture Mancala 1, you should have little trouble learning Basic Crossroads Mancala. The most difficult concepts are understanding the path of play and knowing from whom you capture.

A point new players sometimes miss when learning this game, is that you can double cross capture if your last stone sown lands in your central cup. This means that you can simultaneously capture from the players to your left and right. However, you never capture from the player across from you.

Number of Players: Four

Object: To capture the most stones by the end of the game.

Gameboard: The gameboard is shaped like a large "X", and players sit between two branches of the "X". Each owns the five cups of the section he faces. For you, this would be cups "A" through "E"; for the player to your right, cups "a" through "e"; for the player opposite you, cups "AA" through "EE"; and for the player to your left, cups "aa" through "ee". At the end of each branch is a reservoir. Each player owns the reservoir on his right.

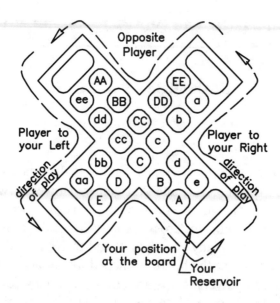

Board Setup: Eighty stones are required. Place four stones in each of the twenty cups, leaving the four reservoirs empty. For a faster game, you may start with three stones per cup.

Playing:

Randomly choose a player to start. Play then progresses to the right. To make a play, take all the stones from any one cup on your section of the board. Sow them all counterclockwise around the board, traveling in right angles as you go. Sow one stone per cup, leaving the cup you originally took the stones from empty. You may sow through all twenty cups plus your reservoir but not the other three players' reservoirs.

Crossroads Mancala uses continued play. (Otherwise, you would not be able to get around the board.) So, after you finish sowing, if the last stone you sow lands in a loaded cup, continue playing. Take the stones from that cup and sow them as before, starting with the next, consecutive cup. Continue sowing around the board in this manner until the last stone sown lands in either your reservoir or an empty cup. (Note: if there are many stones on the board, it is possible you may sow completely around the board and beyond the cup from which you started your play. Be sure to sow a stone into that cup as you pass it.) The figures below illustrate this play, called a continued play.

Assume that the game is in progress and you choose to start your next play from cup "D". Before you make your play, the board looks like this.

The last stone sown lands in cup "B", which already held three stones, and the board now looks like this.

You pick up the stones in cup "B", and, leaving it empty, continue sowing in the same direction. You sow through your reservoir and your last stone sown lands in cup "d". The stones on the board are now arranged like this.

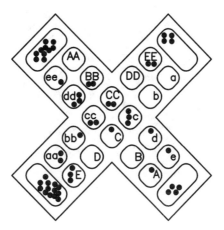

As shown in the figure above, the last of the stones sown landed in cup "d", which was previously empty. Therefore, the continued play ended.

If the last stone you sow lands in your reservoir, you may make another play. Take all the stones from any one cup on your section of the board and sow them as before. If the last stone you sow lands in an empty cup, your turn ends. However, you may be able to capture. If the empty cup is on your section of the board and there is a loaded cup across from it on another player's section of the board, you capture that cup.

Of course, whom you capture from will depend on where your last stone landed. If it landed in one of your left two cups, "D" or "E", you capture the stones from a cup belonging to the player on your left. If it landed in one of your right two cups, "A" or "B", you capture the stones from a cup belonging to the player on your right. In both cases, take the captured stones, plus your last stone sown, and place them in your reservoir. Your turn then ends and the player to your right makes the next play. The following figures illustrate cross capturing as it is used in Crossroads Mancala.

You see that you can capture the stones from the player on your right by starting your play from cup "E". Before you make your play, the board looks like this.

You take all of the stones from cup "E" (leaving it empty) and sow them counterclockwise, starting with cup "D". Your last stone sown lands in cup "B". The board now looks like this.

Since cup "B" was originally empty, and it is across from loaded cup "d", you capture all the stones held in cup "d" plus your last stone sown in cup "B". Take them and place them in your reservoir. The board now looks like this.

If the empty cup your last stone lands in is your central cup "C", you capture any stones held in the central cups of the players next to you. So, if just "c" or "cc" is loaded, you capture the stones held in that cup. If both "cc" and "c" are loaded, you capture the stones held in both cups, called a **double cross capture**. Take your captured stones, plus your last stone sown, and place them in your reservoir. Your turn ends and the player to your right makes the next play. Note, however, that you never capture stones from the central cup of the opposite player. So, if cup "CC" directly across the board is loaded, you must leave the stones where they are. Capturing from cup "C" is illustrated below.

Assume the game is in progress and you start your next play from cup "E". Before you make your play, the board looks this.

Your last stone sown lands in cup "C" as shown in the figure below. Since cup "C" was originally empty, and cups "c" and "cc" are loaded, you capture the stones in "c" and "cc" plus your last stone sown. (Note that a cross capture would still occur if only "c" or "cc" had been loaded.) However, since you may not capture stones from the opposite player, the stones held in cup "CC" remain where they are.

After taking your captured stones and placing them in your reservoir, the board looks like this.

Ending:

Continue playing as described above until all five cups on your section of the board are empty. At this point, you are out of the game. However, you have not necessarily lost, as will be discussed momentarily. The other players will continue to play as before, except they will bypass your cups and your reservoir. This is because your section of the board is removed from the game.

When another player goes empty, she will be out of the game, and her section of the board will also be bypassed. When only one player remains, the game ends. That player takes any stones remaining on the board and places them in his reservoir. The stones are then tallied. The player with the most stones wins. The other players may be ranked by how many stones they have captured.

CROSSROADS MANCALA 2
Nasty Capture

Nasty Capture Crossroads is played like Crossroads Mancala 1, except for the following changes. First, when you make a play, you sow as usual, except rather than bypassing the other three players' reservoirs, you sow through them as you would your own. In most cases, any stones you sow into an opponent's reservoir become part of her winnings. However, if it is your last stone sown, you capture her reservoir. Take all the stones, including your last stone sown, and place them in your reservoir. The following figures illustrate this capture, called the **nasty capture**.

You see that you can capture the reservoir of the player to your right by starting your next play from cup "B". Before you make your play, the board looks like this.

Your last stone sown lands in cup "d", which already held three stones and now holds four. The board now looks like this.

You continue sowing by picking up the stones from cup "d" and sowing them. The last one lands in the reservoir of the player to your right. The board now looks like this.

Because it was your last stone sown that landed in her reservoir, you capture those stones including your last stone sown. You take them and place them in your reservoir. The board now looks like this.

Since this capture can be a nasty blow to another player, especially if she has been building her reservoir for some time, you can see why we call it a nasty capture.

Notes on Strategy:

A lot of the strategy in Nasty Capture Crossroads is centered on being sure that an opponent's reservoir does not get too big. If that is the case, she will instantly win the game if she goes empty. Therefore, it is important that you try to capture her reservoir before this happens.

On the other hand, if you have captured enough stones to win the game, try to go empty. This will put you out of the game, and you will have to wait while the others finish. However, your reservoir will be safe from being captured. Just be sure not to go empty too soon. Wait until you have enough stones to win the game.

Variations:

<u>Play with partners</u>

Nasty Capture Crossroads is well suited to being played with partners. Your partner is the person sitting across from you. Play as instructed above, but work with your partner on strategy. To win the game, you and your partner together must have captured more stones than your two opponents.

African Two-row Games

African mancala board made by authors.

WARI

Wari is the version of mancala that is most often associated with western Africa. Numerous variations are played there for which there are many names such as Woro, Awari, Woli, and Oware. Wari is also found in many other parts of the world, making it perhaps the most widely played version of mancala there is. These places include the Middle East, Central America, South America, Europe, Southeast Asia, and the United States.

Like other African two-row versions, Wari has several features that make it unique. For one thing, you never sow through your reservoir. Reservoirs are only used for storing captured stones. In addition, specific count capturing is used, where you capture cups that originally contained one or two stones. Finally, while played as a single game, Wari is often played in rounds.

Wari is a very old version of mancala. It was probably one of several offshoots of the earliest mancala games introduced to western Africa from Egypt. Centuries later, Wari was taken to the New World by the Africans brought there to work as slaves. In the late 1800s, sociologists studying African culture introduced this version to Europe. It is not certain how Wari reached Southeast Asia, but it most likely also arrived directly from Africa. Today, Wari is popular with Americans. It appears as computer games and games sold by major game manufacturers and artisans.

Included in this chapter are several variations of Wari. The games of One-round Wari and Wari Rounds follow typical rules. Following these games are three less common African variations.

ONE-ROUND WARI
The Basic Game

One-round Wari is a variation of Wari that is popular with American mancala players. This may surprise you, since at first glance it appears very simple. There is no continued play, and since plays are not made through the reservoir, there are no go-again plays. You simply sow one cup of stones and your turn ends. Depending on where your last stone sown landed, you may or may not capture.

In spite of its simplicity, though, One-round Wari is strategically quite interesting. This is because of series capturing, a play that allows you to capture more than one of your opponent's cups on a single play. You are even allowed to capture all six, clearing her side. This is called a grand capture and it ends the game, giving you not only your captured stones but also any remaining on your side. Series and grand captures are not easy to make, though, especially among equally matched players. That is where the challenge lies in this otherwise simple game.

Object: To capture more stones than your opponent by the end of the game.

Gameboard: The gameboard consists of two rows of six cups and may have, but does not require, two reservoirs at each end for storing stones captured during the game. Each player owns the row of six cups nearest him. Thus, your cups would be cups "A" through "F" and your opponent's cups, "a" through "f" as seen in the figure below. Since stones are not sown through the reservoir, which reservoir you own is not important. Traditionally, however, players use the reservoir on their right.

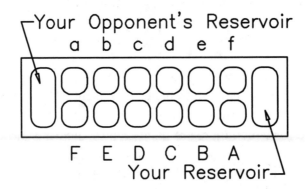

Board Setup: Forty-eight stones are required. Place four stones in each of the twelve cups, leaving the two reservoirs empty.

Playing:

Randomly choose a player to start. To make a play, take all the stones from any one of your six cups and sow them all counterclockwise around the board. Sow one stone per cup starting with the cup next to the one from which you originally took the stones. You may sow through all twelve cups, but do not sow through either reservoir. The following figures illustrate this play, called the single play.

Assume that the game is in progress and you choose to start your play from cup "D". Before you make your play, the board looks like this.

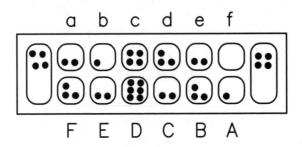

You pick up all six stones from cup "D", leaving it empty, and then sow one stone each into cups "C", "B", and "A". You skip your reservoir and continue sowing onto your opponent's side, starting with cup "f" and continuing with cup "e". Your last stone sown lands in cup "d", and the play ends with the board looking like this.

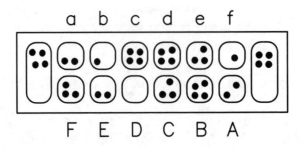

Once you finish sowing, your turn ends, but you may be able to make a specific-count capture. If the last stone you sow lands in a cup on your opponent's side of the board that originally held either one or two stones and now holds two or three, you capture those stones. If the preceding cup and any consecutive cups before it also hold two or three stones and are on your opponent's side, you capture those stones as well. This is an example of a series capture. In this game, you capture the stones from all cups in the series, even if you clear your opponent's side (a grand capture). Take your captured stones and store them in your reservoir. Capturing and series capturing are illustrated below.

Assume that the game is in progress and you see that if you start your next play from cup "C", you will be able to make a capture. Before you make your play, the board looks like this.

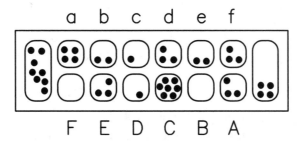

Your last stone sown landed in cup "b", which originally held two stones but now holds three. You capture those stones including your last stone sown. Move them to your reservoir for storage. Additionally, since cup "c", preceding the captured cup, also holds two stones and is on your opponent's side, you capture those stones as well. Take them and move them to your reservoir.

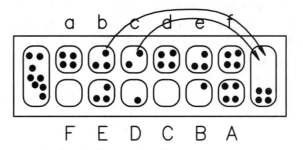

After you move your captured stones from cups "b" and "c" to your reservoir, the board looks like this.

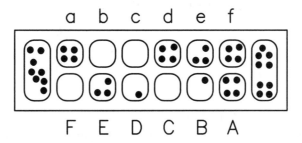

You may have noticed that cup "e" on your opponent's side also holds three stones. However, it is not available for series capture. This is because it is separated from the other two cups by a cup holding four stones, interrupting the series. Therefore, you do not capture cup "e", even though it meets the other criteria for series capturing. Your opponent makes the next play.

Ending:

The game ends when it is your opponent's turn and she can no longer play because

- You made a play that cleared her side
- She made a play that cleared her side and you can play nothing to her on your next turn

You capture all the stones that remain on your side. Move them to your reservoir. However, if your opponent makes a play that clears her side, and you can play something to her on your next turn, the game continues.

Sometimes a game will reach a stalemate where no more captures are possible and to continue playing would be pointless. In this instance, players may agree to end the game and keep any stones remaining on their side. The player with more captured stones at the end of the game wins.

Variations:

<u>When sowing, skip over the cup from which you started</u>

In some variations of Wari, if you have enough stones to sow completely around the board or beyond, you skip over the cup from which you started. For instance, if you start your play from cup "C" and it contained twelve or more stones, you would sow one stone per cup until you reached cup "C". You would then skip cup "C" and continue sowing starting with cup "B".

Notes on Strategy:

The strategy for Wari is to hoard as many stones as possible on your side of the board. This allows you to control the game, and set your opponent up for a series capture, or better yet, a grand capture. Grand captures take extra planning, however. They usually occur only when you can sow a cup full of stones more than once around the board. At the same time your opponent's cups should be empty or contain only one stone.

WARI ROUNDS
A Traditional African Form

Wari is often played in rounds, especially in Africa. The object of any individual round is the same as for One-round Wari, to capture as many stones as possible. However, the ultimate goal of the match is to leave your opponent unable to play, because you have captured most or all of her cups.

For the first round, play as described under One-round Wari. For the second round, take all your captured stones and, starting from your reservoir and moving left, place four per cup in as many of your cups as you can. If you fill all your cups and have stones left over, continue clockwise around the board, filling your opponent's cups with four stones. If you are down to three or fewer stones, return them to your reservoir, even though an empty cup will remain on the board.

Any cups you fill, including those on your opponent's side, are yours for the round. If you find it difficult to keep track of them, place a marker beside them to help you remember where they are. (Of course, a native player would never do this, as any decent player should be able to memorize his cups!) If any cup is empty, it goes to the player with fewer cups. Start the new round with the person who now has fewer cups. You may start a play from any cup you now own and capture from any cups that your opponent now owns.

At the beginning of a new round, place the stones in your reservoir back in the cups as you did in round two. Cups lost during the previous round may be taken back if enough stones were captured. Then play as before.

Rounds are repeated until one player is left with fewer than four stones and therefore has no cups. However, once either player is down to three cups, it is almost impossible to recover and players usually agree to end the game there. The player who owns more cups wins the game.

Variations:

Choose the cups you take on a new round

When setting up for a new round, after you fill your own cups, you may choose the cups you take from your opponent. As before, any cups you fill with four stones, including those on your opponent's side, are yours for the round. Place a marker beside each of the cups you own if you need help remembering them.

Start the new round with the player whose turn was second on the previous round. Play as directed above, trying to win enough stones to gain as many cups as possible for the next round.

Playing with three or four players

Because the object is to capture more cups rather than more stones, Wari Rounds may be played with up to four players. Players each start with an equal number of adjacent cups. If necessary, a longer board may be used to accommodate more players. As the game progresses, players are eliminated once they lose all of their cups. When the game is down to the last two players, they continue until one loses enough of her cups to make continuing pointless. The winner is the remaining player.

CHILDREN'S WARI
A Simplified Variation of One-round Wari

Children's Wari is an African variation of Wari that, as the name implies, is designed for children. It is played like One-round Wari, but series capturing has been eliminated. In addition, the object has been simplified. In Children's Wari, the object is to capture a designated number of stones before your opponent. This number is usually twenty-five, half plus one of the stones, but players may agree on a smaller total before the game begins.

Children's Wari continues until one player has captured the designated number (or more) of stones, that player being the winner. If one player's side of the board goes empty before this, the player without stones on his side passes until his opponent plays something to his side. The opponent must do so as soon as she can.

AYO
Wari with Continued Play

Ayo is a variation of Wari played by the Yoruba people of Nigeria. Its rules are nearly the same as One-round Wari, but there are several notable differences. For one thing, Ayo has continued play. So, after you finish sowing, if the last stone you sow lands in any loaded cup, and it is not a cup you can capture, continue playing. Take the stones from that cup and sow them as you normally would, starting with the next cup as you move counterclockwise. Continue sowing in this manner until the last stone lands in either an empty cup or a cup you can capture (one on your opponent's side that already held one or two stones and now holds two or three). The continued play is shown in the figures below.

Assume that the game is in progress, and you choose to start your next play from cup "F". Before you make your play, the board looks like this.

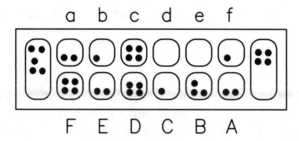

Your last stone sown lands in cup "B", which contains three stones and the board now looks like this.

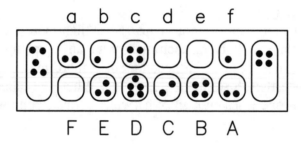

Since you can not capture the stones in cup "B", pick them up, including your last stone sown, and sow them in the same direction. The stones on the board are now arranged like this.

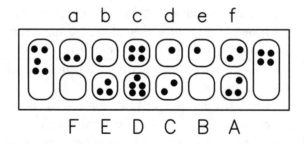

As seen in the figure above, the last of the stones played landed in cup "d", which was previously empty, and the continued play ended.

Capturing in Ayo is the same as in One-round Wari, and there is series capturing. However, since you may not take the last cup in a series if it would clear your opponent's side, there is no grand capturing (although you may clear your opponent's side on a regular one-cup capture). In addition, Ayo ends when the entire board is empty of all stones rather than just your opponent's side as in Wari. If one player's side goes empty before this happens, he passes until his opponent plays something to his side. The opponent must do so at the first opportunity.

Sometimes Ayo may reach a stalemate. In this instance, players may agree to end the game and keep any stones remaining on their side. The player with more captured stones at the end of the game wins.

Comments:

The original instructions stated that if you have enough stones to sow completely around the board and beyond, you skip over the cup from which you started. While this works well for single play games, we found it was rather pointless in continued play games. However, include it if you like.

Notes on Strategy:

Ayo is similar to Wari in many ways, but the two games play very differently in terms of strategy. Because continued play constantly mixes the stones, it is more difficult to make a series capture, and there will be fewer cups in the series. In addition, since the game continues until the entire board is empty, you can not rely on forcing your opponent to go empty and keeping what is left on your side to win the game. This makes Ayo more dependent on luck than Wari.

Playing in Rounds: Ayo may be played in rounds using the rules for Wari Rounds.

J'ODU
A Cross Capture Variation of Wari

J'odu is another variation of Wari played by the Yoruba people. It is played like Ayo, except the game starts with three stones per cup instead of four. Second, capturing is somewhat different. You do not capture by landing your last stone in an opponent's cup containing one or two stones. Instead, your last stone must land in an empty cup on your side of the board. This cup must be directly across from a cup on your opponent's side containing one or two stones. This type of capture is called a **specific-count cross capture**.

There is series capturing in J'odu, so if the preceding cup and any consecutive cups before it on your opponent's side, also hold one or two stones, you capture those stones as well. However, since you may not take the last cup in a series if it would clear your opponent's side, there is no grand capturing (although you may clear your opponent's side on a regular one-cup capture). Specific-count cross capturing is illustrated below.

Assume the game is in progress. You see that if you start your next play from cup "E", you can capture the stones held in your opponent's cup "e". Before you make your play, the board looks like this.

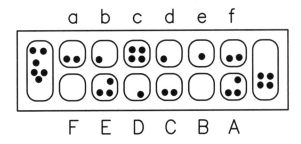

You pick up the stones from cup "E", and leaving it empty, sow them one by one into the adjacent cups. Your last stone sown lands in cup "B", which was previously empty. Since cup "B" is across from cup "e" on your opponent's side and cup "e" contains one stone, you make a capture. Additionally, since cup "f" preceding the captured cup holds two stones and is on your opponent's side, you capture those stones as well.

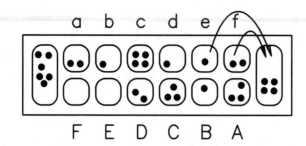

Take the stones from cups "e" and "f" but not your last stone sown and place them in your reservoir. After you take the stones, the board looks like this.

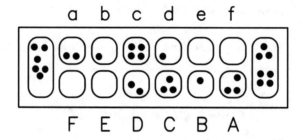

Your turn ends and your opponent makes the next play.

Comments:

J'odu as originally written did not play well, so we modified several rules. First, we reduced the number of stones the game started with from four per cup to three per cup. We found with four stones per cup no combinations occurred that you could capture. Second, we dropped the rule: if you have enough stones to sow completely around the board and beyond, skip over the cup from which you started. This was because if you skipped over the cup, you could not capture from it. With almost no other cups to capture from, especially at the beginning, the game became almost deadlocked.

Notes on Strategy:

This game (originally intended for women and children) does not have the strategic challenge of other variations of Wari. This is because continued play makes it somewhat a game of luck, especially at the beginning where there are many stones on the board. Continued play imposes limits on series capturing as well. Still, the game has its own attraction, once enough stones are cleared off the board. This is because the style of capturing requires an unusual strategy for a Wari game.

Playing in Rounds: J'odu may be played in rounds using the rules for Wari Rounds.

Hand-carved African Wari board from authors' collection.

ADI

ADI IS A version of mancala played in western and northern Africa. It is almost as popular as Wari and at first glance appears to be a variation. However, Adi differs in several ways. Like Wari, Adi uses specific-count capturing. However, in Adi the cup must have originally held three stones, rather than one or two as in Wari. In addition, you may capture any cup on the board, whereas in Wari it must be on your opponent's side. Finally, in Adi there is no series capturing, although there is another form of bonus capturing called passing-fours.

Concerning its history, Adi has been played in northern and western Africa for hundreds of years and is probably another offshoot of the earliest mancala games played there. It is thought to be even older than Wari. Like Wari, Adi has found its way to many other parts of the world, including Central America and Southeast Asia. It is played to some extent in the United States, although it is not as popular as Cross Capture Mancala or Wari.

Included in this chapter are several variations of Adi. The first three are traditional African forms. The chapter ends with two non-African variations, one from the United States and one from Southeast Asia.

ONE-ROUND ADI
The Basic Game

One-round Adi is a basic form of Adi. It has continued play, so you sow until your last stone sown lands in either an empty cup or one containing three stones. In the latter case, you capture. If you want more challenge, you can add capturing of passing-fours, which is discussed as a variation.

Object: To capture more stones than your opponent by the end of the game.

Gameboard: The gameboard consists of two rows of six cups and may have, but does not require, two reservoirs at each end for storing stones captured during the game. Each player owns the row of six cups nearest him. Thus, your cups would be cups "A" through "F" and your opponent's cups, "a" through "f" as shown in the figure below. Since stones are not sown through the reservoir, which reservoir you own is not important. Traditionally, however, players use the reservoir on their right.

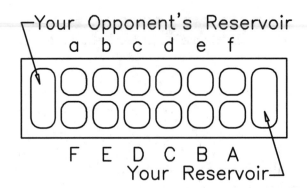

Board Setup: Forty-eight stones are required. Place four stones in each of the twelve cups, leaving the two reservoirs empty.

Playing:

Randomly choose a player to start. To make a play, take all the stones from any one of your six cups and sow them all counterclockwise around the board. Sow one stone per cup, starting with the cup next to the one from which you originally took the stones. You may sow through all twelve cups, but do not sow through either reservoir.

If the last stone you sow lands in an empty cup on either side of the board, your turn ends and your opponent makes the next play. If your last stone sown lands in a loaded cup containing any number of stones other than three, continue playing. Take the stones from that cup and sow them as described above, starting with the next cup. Continue sowing in this manner until the last stone lands in either an empty cup or a cup holding three stones. This is called a continued play and is illustrated below.

Assume that the game is in progress, and you choose to start your next play from cup "F". Before you make your play, the board looks like this.

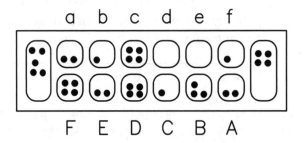

Your last stone sown lands in cup "B", which originally held four stones, and the board now looks like this.

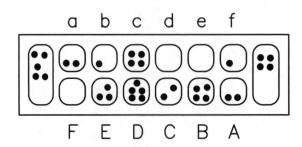

68

You then pick up the stones in cup "B", including your last stone sown, and sow them in the same direction. The stones on the board are now arranged like this.

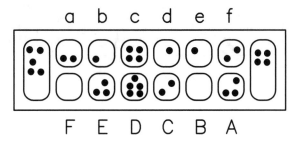

As seen in the figure above, the last stone sown landed in cup "d". This cup was previously empty, and the continued play ended.

After you finish sowing, if the last stone lands in a cup on either side of the board that already held three stones and now holds four, you capture the four stones. Take them and place them in your reservoir. Your turn then ends and your opponent makes the next play. Specific-count capturing as used in Adi is illustrated below.

Assume that the game is in progress and you see that if you start your next play from cup "C", you will be able to make a capture. Before you make this play, the board looks like this.

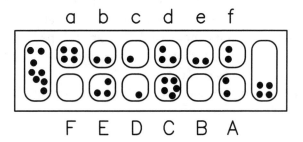

You pick up all the stones from cup "C" and sow one each into cups "B" and "A". You bypass your reservoir and continue with cups "f" and "e" on your opponent's side. Your last stone sown lands in cup "d". Now the board looks like this.

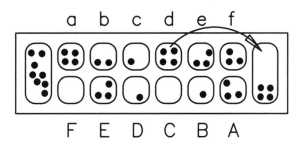

Since cup "d" originally held three stones and your last stone sown made its total four, you capture those stones. Take them and place them in your reservoir for storage. The board now looks like this.

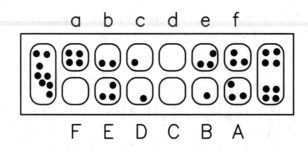

Ending:

The game continues until there are only eight stones remaining on the board. The first player to capture four of the eight automatically gets the remaining four, clearing the board and ending the game. The player with more stones wins.

If one player's side goes empty before the board is cleared, he passes until his opponent plays something to his side. The opponent is not obligated to do this immediately, however, and may leave the first player stranded for a time if she likes.

Variations:

Add passing-fours

Play as instructed above except for the following change. If you sow a stone, <u>other than your last</u>, into a cup that held three stones and make its total four, the cup becomes a passing-four. In this game, you may capture a passing-four, but only if you are the person sowing, and only if it is on your side of the board. Any passing-fours that form on your opponent's side are not available to you for capture. Capturing of passing-fours is illustrated below.

Assume that the game is in progress and you start your next play from cup "C". Before you make this play, the board looks like this.

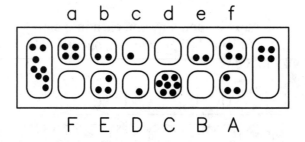

You pick up all the stones from cup "C" and sow one each into cups "B" and "A". You pause, hanging on to the other stones from "C", because cup "A" that originally held three stones now has four, becoming a passing-four as shown below.

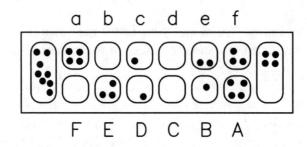

Since cup "A" is on your side of the board and you are the one sowing, you capture the stones held in it. Take them and place them in your reservoir. The board now looks like this.

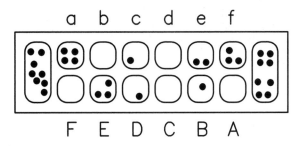

You resume sowing the rest of the stones you took from cup "C", starting with cup "f". Cup "f" also becomes a passing-four. You may not capture it, though, because it is on your opponent's side. You therefore finish sowing the remaining stones. As shown below, your last stone sown lands in cup "b". Since cup "b" was originally empty, your turn ends and your opponent makes the next play.

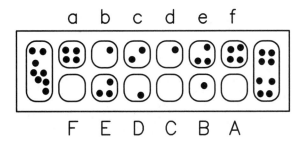

Note: the stones in a passing-four must be taken immediately. If a fifth stone is sown into the cup, it is no longer a passing-four and may not be captured. Some players require that the passing-four be taken before the next cup of stones is picked up.

Notes on Strategy:

Because of continued play and passing-fours, One-round Adi is somewhat a game of luck, especially toward the beginning when there are many stones on the board. As the game progresses and there are fewer stones on the board there is more control over the strategy.

ADI ROUNDS
A Traditional African Form

The Ewe people of Ghana play Adi, which they traditionally play in rounds. When played in rounds, Adi becomes much more challenging, because of a change to the object of the game. For individual rounds, the object is still to capture more stones than your opponent. (In fact, you want to capture as many stones as possible in order to own as many cups as possible.) The overall goal, though, is to disable your opponent by capturing all or most of her cups. In this way, you eventually hope to leave her unable to play.

For the first round, play as described under One-round Adi. For the second round, take your captured stones and, starting from your reservoir and moving left, place four per cup in as many of your cups as you can. If you fill all your cups and have stones left over, continue clockwise around the board, filling cups on your opponent's side with four stones. Any cups you fill, including those on your opponent's side, are yours for this round. You may start a play from any of these cups.

Mark them if you need to. (Of course, capturing will not be affected since you capture from cups on either side of the board in this game, no matter who owns them.) Play as before, starting with the person who went second in the previous round.

At the beginning of the next round, place your captured stones back in the cups as you did in round two. Cups lost during the previous round can be taken back if enough stones were captured. Then play as before.

Rounds are repeated until one player is left with no stones, and thus can not retain ownership of any cups. However, once either player is down to three or fewer cups, it is almost impossible to recover. Therefore, at this point players usually agree to end the game. The player who owns more cups wins.

Variations:

Choose the cups you take on a new round

For a new round, once you fill your own cups, you may choose the cups you take from your opponent. As usual, any cups you fill, including those on your opponent's side, are yours for the round. Place a marker beside each of the cups you own if you need help remembering them.

Start the new round with the player whose turn was second on the previous round. Play as directed for round one, trying to win enough stones to gain as many cups as possible for the next round.

Playing with three or four players

An interesting feature of Adi Rounds is that, because the object is to capture more cups than your opponent rather than more stones, it may be played with up to four players. Players each start with an equal number of adjacent cups. If necessary, a board with more cups per row may be used to accommodate the extra players. As the game progresses, the first two players to lose all of their cups are eliminated. When the game is down to the last two players, they play until one finally loses all his cups or enough to make continuing pointless. The winner is the player with the most cups.

BA-AWA
Adi with Passing-fours

Ba-awa is a variation of Adi played by the Twi people of Ghana. It is played like One-round Adi with passing-fours, but it differs in how capturing and passing-fours are handled. In Ba-awa it is not the person sowing who captures, but the owner of the cup. This means that if your last stone sown lands in a cup on your side of the board that already held three stones and now holds four, you capture. Take the four stones and place them in your reservoir. However, if the cup is on your opponent's side of the board, she captures, taking the four stones and placing them in her reservoir.

Capturing of passing-fours follows a similar pattern. If a passing-four forms on your side of the board, you take those stones and place them in your reservoir. However, if it forms on your opponent's side, she takes the stones and places them in her reservoir. Again, it does not matter who is sowing.

As in Adi, the stones in a passing-four must be taken immediately. Once there are five stones in a passing-four, it may no longer be captured. Optionally, you may also require that the passing-four be taken before the next cup of stones is picked up.

Notes on Strategy:

You will naturally want to avoid plays where the last stone sown lands in a cup on your opponent's side that contains three stones, allowing her to capture. This will initially be difficult to do, as this game has continued play, constantly mixing the stones. However, as the game progresses and stones thin out, you should have more control over your plays.

Playing in Rounds:

Ba-awa is traditionally played in rounds using the same rules as Adi Rounds. Any variation used in Adi Rounds may be used for this game.

FOUR-CAPTURE
An American Variation of Adi

Four-capture is a variation of Adi taught to us by an American player. It is played like Adi, except for the following changes. First, after your first turn, you may choose your direction of play. This means that you must sow counterclockwise on your first turn. After that, however, you may sow either clockwise or counterclockwise on any turn, although you may not change directions during a single turn. The same rules apply to your opponent.

Four-capture also ends differently than Adi. Rather than ending when the entire board is cleared, the game ends when you make a play and all of your cups go empty, and your opponent can not sow anything to your side on her next move. You then capture all the stones remaining in your opponent's cups. Take the stones and place them in your reservoir. However, if your opponent is able to sow something onto your side, the game continues. She must do so on her next play.

Comments:

This go-empty ending is unusual for an Adi variation. It was probably adapted from an American Cross Capture game. While it makes for an interesting variation, it precludes any possibility of playing in rounds. This is because it would be too easy for the player with fewer cups to capture his opponent's cups. Games would bounce back and forth and never end. However, a disable ending works for rounds. In a disable ending, the game ends when it is your opponent's turn and she can no longer play because her side of the board is empty. You capture the stones that remain on your side and add them to your winnings.

Notes on Strategy:

Choosing your direction of sowing on any turn has some advantages. For one thing, it is easier to capture, since you can attack from either direction. However, keep in mind your opponent has the same advantage.

MOTIQ
An Indonesian Variation of Adi

The Kedang people of Eastern Indonesia play Motiq. It is played similarly to Adi with the following differences. First, Motiq ends differently. It does not end when the entire board is cleared. It ends when one player goes empty and the other can not sow anything to the first player's side on her next turn. The player who went empty then captures all the stones remaining in his opponent's cups. Of course, if your opponent is able to sow a stone into one of your cups, the game continues. She must do so on her next play.

Second, Motiq allows a capture go-again play. That is, after you capture, your turn does not end if there are stones in the cup immediately following the one from which you just captured. Instead, you may make another play by picking up those stones and sowing them around the board.

If you again capture, the same rules again apply. There is no limit on how many capture go-again plays you may make during the same turn.

Comments:

The original instructions for this game called for a gameboard with seven cups per rows instead of six. However, it plays just as well on a six-cup board. Also, as with Four-capture, the go-empty ending, which probably was adapted from a local Sungka variation, precludes playing in rounds. However, here, too, you can substitute a disable ending if you wish to play in rounds. Again, in a disable ending, the game ends when it is your opponent's turn and she can no longer play because her side of the board is empty. You capture the stones that remain on your side and add them to your winnings.

Notes on Strategy:

The capture go-again play is interesting, but may lead to the first player "cleaning up" while the second player gets no chance to play. This is more likely at the beginning of the game when there are many stones on the board. Try the game as instructed. If you find that the capture go-again play gets out of hand, try limiting it to one extra turn or adding the passing-fours variation (described under One-round Adi) to compensate.

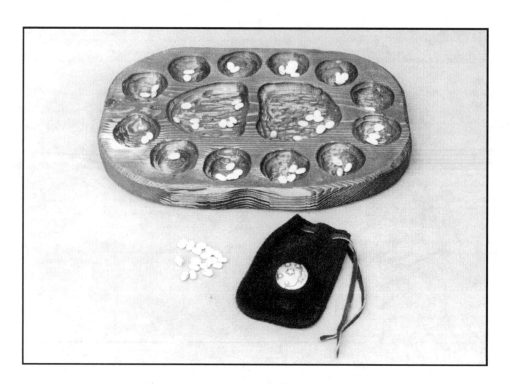

Middle Eastern style mancala board made by authors.

MANKALA'H

MANKALA'H IS A version of mancala played in northeastern Africa and the Middle East that is similar to Wari. Like Wari, it uses specific-count capturing and series capturing is also allowed. However, to capture in Mankala'h, your last stone sown must land in a cup containing one or three stones instead of one or two. In addition, this cup may be on either side of the board, not just on your opponent's side. Finally, Mankala'h traditionally starts with a strategic setup where one player sets up the board. Wari begins with a fixed setup, usually four stones per cup.

Mankala'h is an ancient game. Like other African two-row versions, it is probably a direct descendant of the earliest mancala games played in Egypt. Mankala'h is also the first version of mancala to be documented by a European, an Englishman named Edward Lane. It is from his work in the 1800s that the name mancala was adopted to refer to the family of count and capture games.

Included in this chapter is the traditional Egyptian game of Mankala'h. Following this is an American variation called Mankala and Mangala, a game played in Sudan.

ONE-ROUND MANKALA'H
The Basic Game

One-round Mankala'h is a good game to start with when learning Mankala'h. For one thing, fewer stones are required, so it plays faster. In addition, a fixed setup has been substituted for the strategic setup. Finally, it is played as a single game rather than in rounds.

Object: To capture more stones than your opponent by the end of the game.

Gameboard: The gameboard consists of two rows of six cups and may have, but does not require, two reservoirs at each end for storing stones captured during the game. Each player owns the row of six cups nearest him. Thus, your cups would be cups "A" through "F" and your opponent's cups, "a" through "f" as shown in the figure below. Since stones are not sown through the reservoir, which reservoir you own is not important. Traditionally, however, players use the reservoir on their right.

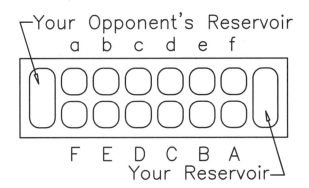

Board Setup: Forty-eight stones are required. Place four stones in each of the twelve cups, leaving the two reservoirs empty.

Playing:

Randomly choose a player to start. To make a play, take all the stones from any one of your six cups and sow them all counterclockwise around the board. Sow one stone per cup starting with the cup next to the one from which you originally took the stones. You may sow through all twelve cups, but do not sow through either reservoir.

If the last stone you sow lands in an empty cup on either side of the board, your turn ends and your opponent makes the next play. If the last stone you sow lands in a cup on either side of the board that already held two, four, or more stones and now holds three, five, or more, continue playing. Take the stones from that cup and sow them as described above, starting with the next cup. Continue sowing in this manner until your last stone lands in either an empty cup or a cup that already held one or three stones. This is called a continued play and is shown in the figures below.

Assume that the game is in progress, and you choose to start your next play from cup "F". Before you make your play, the board looks like this.

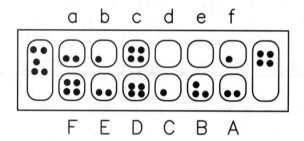

Your last stone sown lands in cup "B", which originally held four stones and the board now looks like this.

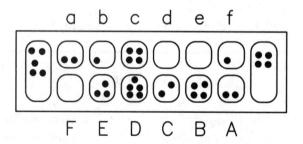

You then pick up the stones in cup "B", including your last stone sown, and sow them in the same direction. The stones on the board are now arranged like this.

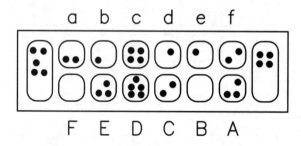

78

As seen in the figure above, the last stone sown landed in cup "d". This cup was previously empty, and the continued play ended.

Once you finish sowing, if the last stone lands in a cup on either side of the board, and that cup already held one or three stones and now holds two or four, you capture those stones. This is called a specific-count capture. If the preceding cup and any consecutive cups before it also contain two or four stones, you capture those stones as well, called a series capture. (Note that in Mankala'h a series capture may continue onto the other side of the board.) Take your captured stones and place them in your reservoir. Your opponent makes the next play. Capturing and series capturing are shown in the figures below.

Assume that the game is in progress and you see that if you start your next play from cup "C", you will be able to make a capture. Before you make your play, the board looks like this.

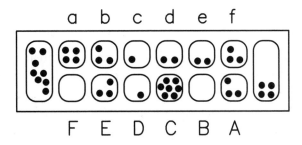

Your last stone sown landed in cup "b", which originally held three stones but now holds four. You capture those stones plus your last stone sown. Move them to your reservoir for storage. Note, however, that you do not capture the stones in cup "f" or cup "A". This is because they are separated from the other cups in the series by two cups holding three stones.

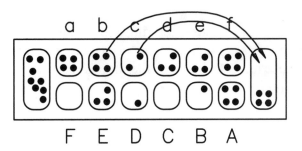

After you move your captured stones from cups "b" and "c" to your reservoir, the board looks like this.

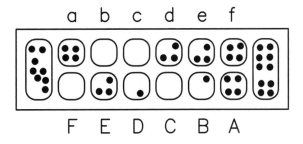

Your opponent then makes the next play.

Since series capturing can continue around the entire board in Mankala'h, you can potentially capture all twelve cups. Unfortunately, even small series captures are difficult to make and capturing the entire board is nearly impossible. This is because continued play makes it difficult to create a lineup of cups containing one or three stones.

Ending:

The game ends when no stones remain on the board. If one player's side goes empty before this happens, the opponent must choose and place any one of the stones on her side in the first player's leftmost cup and the game continues.

In some cases, the game will reach a stalemate, usually when the board is down to two stones. If this occurs, players may do one of two things, which they must agree upon before starting the game. They may end the game and split the remaining stones or the first player who gets both stones on his side captures them. In all cases, once the game ends, the player who has captured more stones wins.

Variations:

Capture go-again

Play as directed above, except whenever you capture, you may start a new play. In some variations, you may start this play from any one cup on your side of the board. In others, however, you only have this freedom until you make your first capture. After that, your go-again play must start from the first loaded cup left of your reservoir. There is no limit on how many go-again plays you may make during the same turn.

Add bonus capturing

Play as directed above, except when you make a single or series capture additionally take all the stones from any adjacent cups that are on the opposite side of the board. Place them in your reservoir.

Comments:

Capture go-again plays and bonus capturing are interesting variations, but they generally give one player too much of an advantage. We suggest that if you include the capture go-again, restrict players to one extra turn. Regarding the bonus capturing, we dropped it altogether. However, try a few games and see how you like it.

MANKALA'H ROUNDS
A Traditional Egyptian Form

Mankala'h Rounds is the traditional form of Mankala'h played in Egypt. It is played by mostly the same rules as One-round mancala and may use any of its variations. The object of any one round is still to capture more stones than your opponent by the end of the game. The ultimate goal over a series of rounds, however, is to be the first player to reach a score of sixty.

Seventy-two stones are required. For the first round, choose a player to set up the board. Without counting, this player should place about half the stones on each player's side of the board in any cups he chooses. The other player makes the first play. If she does not like the way the first player set up the board, she may turn the board around. However, she forfeits her right to go first. After this, play as described in One-round Mankala'h. Score the game as described below.

For Subsequent Rounds, play as you did for the first round, except the player who won the previous round sets up the board. In some variations, the player to set up the board is the one who did not set it up in the last round.

Scoring:

Score each round as follows. When a round ends, each player counts his captured stones. If players have captured an equal number of stones, the game is a draw and no one scores. Otherwise, the winner of the round (the one with more captured stones) calculates his score by counting the number of stones he has captured and subtracting from it the number of stones his opponent has captured. For instance, if the winner captured thirty-eight stones and his opponent captured ten, the winner's score would be twenty-eight for that round.

Once you calculate your score for the round, add it to a running tally. Remember that the loser scores nothing even though he has captured stones. The player to reach sixty points first wins the match.

MANKALA
An American Variation

Mankala is a game included in an American book of African games. It is unquestionably a variation of Mankala'h but has a variation of capturing that may have been influenced by an American Cross Capture game.

Forty stones are required. A strategic setup is used with one player placing two to five stones in each of the twelve cups on the board. The board does not have to be set up symmetrically, but each player should start with about half the stones on his side. The other player makes the first play. If she does not like the way the board is set up, she may turn the board around, but she gives up her right to go first. After the board is set up, play as described in One-round Mankala'h except for the following changes to capturing and ending the game.

To capture, the last stone you sow must land in a cup on either side of the board that already held one or three stones and now holds two or four. However, you do not capture the stones from the cup where your last stone landed. Instead, you capture the stones in the adjacent cup on the opposite side of the board. Take them and place them in your reservoir. Your turn now ends.

The game ends when both players agree that there are too few stones to make any more significant plays. Players keep any stones remaining on their side. If one player's side goes empty before this happens, he passes until his opponent plays something to his side. She must do so at her first opportunity. The player with more captured stones at the end of the game wins.

Comments:

In the original instructions, you are restricted to starting all of your plays from the first loaded cup to the left of your reservoir. In addition, the game is single play. We felt both of these rules resulted in a predictable game with little strategy. As always, though, try them and see what you like.

Playing in Rounds: Mankala may be played in rounds using the rules for Mankala'h Rounds.

MANGALA
Mankala'h with an African Four-row Influence

The Baggara people of northern Sudan play Mangala. It is played similarly to One-round Mankala'h but has several differences. First, the game is played bi-directionally using single play. Second, you may not start a play from a cup holding a singleton (one stone). Finally, the game ends when one player's side of the board is empty of all stones or only has cups holding singletons. These latter two rules are probably an influence of a local four-row version.

Sixty stones are required and a fixed setup is used. Place five stones in each of the twelve cups on the board, leaving the reservoirs empty. To make a play, take all the stones from any one of your six cups containing at least two stones. You may never start a play from a cup containing a singleton. The direction you sow will depend on which cup you selected. If you start from one of your rightmost cups, cups "A" through "C", you sow counterclockwise. If you start from one of your leftmost cups, cups "D" through "F", you sow clockwise. This is the case for every turn, and it is shown in the figure below.

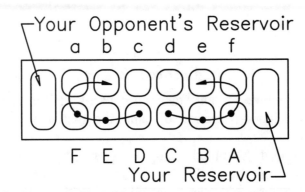

No matter what direction you sow, sow all the stones you picked up. Sow around the board, one stone per cup, starting with the cup next to the one from which you originally took the stones. Do not change directions during sowing. You may sow through all twelve cups, but do not sow through either reservoir. Since this is a single play game, when you finish sowing your first cup of stones, your turn ends. There are no changes to capturing. Capturing in Mangala is done as in One-round Mankala'h.

The game ends when one player can not make a play, because all of his cups are empty or contain singletons. Players keep any stones remaining on their side. The player with more captured stones at the end of the game wins.

Variations:

<u>Add continued play</u>

Play as directed, except for the following change. If your last stone sown lands in a cup on either side of the board that already held two, four, or more stones and now holds three, five, or more, continue playing. Take the stones from that cup and sow them as described above, starting with the next cup. Sow in the same direction you were sowing before. Do not change directions, no matter what cup your continued play starts from. Continue sowing in this manner until your last stone lands in either an empty cup, ending your turn, or a cup that already held one or three stones, whereby you capture.

<u>Add series capturing</u>

Play as directed above, except when you capture, if the preceding cup and any consecutive cups before it also contain two or four stones, you capture the stones held in those cups as well. Take the captured stones and place them in your reservoir.

Playing in Rounds: Mangala may be played in rounds using the rules for Mankala'h Rounds.

Asian Two-row Games

Pallanguli board with center reservoirs made by authors.

PALLANGULI: INDIAN MANCALA

Pallanguli IS A version of mancala played in India and Sri Lanka. Somewhat of a transition version, it has characteristics of games played in both Africa and Southeast Asia. Like African versions, you never sow through your reservoir. Reservoirs are only used for storing captured stones. In addition, a type of secondary capture similar to that used in Adi is allowed. Like Southeast Asian games, Pallanguli is played on a board with seven cups per row and starts with five or more stones per cup. In addition, it is played in rounds where players' cups become active and inactive, depending on the number of stones captured at the end of the previous round.

While Pallanguli has many features in common with African and Asian versions, it is unique regarding sowing and capturing. This is because in Pallanguli your plays are not determined by the cup where your last stone lands but by the cups that follow. How this unusual style of sowing and capturing developed is not clear as no related version can be identified. Thus, we speculate that Pallaguli's style of sowing and capturing is an Indian development.

Pallanguli goes by many names, such as Pallankuli and Pallam Kuzhi, which would lead you to believe it also has many variations. Interestingly, though, while names abound, most games have nearly the same rules. Therefore, we have combined them under one basic heading, Pallanguli. We were able to find three slightly different variations, however. These follow Pallanguli Rounds.

ONE-ROUND PALLANGULI
The Basic Game

One-round Pallanguli is a simplified form of traditional Pallanguli that is played as a single game rather than in Rounds. In addition, passing-fours, a secondary form of capture, has been made a variation. In this way, you can concentrate on learning the basic game.

Object: To capture more stones than your opponent by the end of the game.

Gameboard: The gameboard consists of two rows of seven cups and a reservoir at each end for storing stones captured during the game. Players each own half the cups. Your cups would be cups "A" through "G" and your opponent's cups, "a" through "g" as shown below. Since stones are not sown through the reservoir, which reservoir you own is not important. Traditionally, though, players use the reservoir on their right.

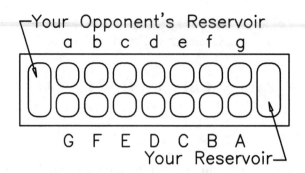

Board Setup: Fifty-six stones are required. Place four stones in each of the fourteen cups, leaving the two reservoirs empty.

Playing:

Randomly choose a player to start. To make a play, take all the stones from any one of your seven cups and sow them all counterclockwise around the board. Sow one stone per cup starting with the cup next to the one from which you originally took the stones. You may sow through all fourteen cups, but do not sow through either reservoir.

In Pallanguli, it is not the cup where your last stone lands, but the cups following it that determine your next action. So, if your last stone lands in a cup on either side of the board followed by a loaded cup, continue playing. However, do not take any stones from the cup where your last stone landed. Instead, take the stones from the cup following it. Then, leaving that cup empty, sow the stones as you did before, starting with the cup following the one from which you took the stones. You continue sowing in this manner until the last stone you sow lands in a cup followed by an empty cup. This play is called a next-cup continued play, and it is illustrated by the figures below.

Assume the game is in progress, and you choose to start your next play from cup "E". Before you make your play, the board looks like this.

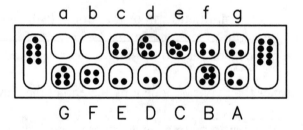

The last stone you sow lands in cup "C". The board now looks like this.

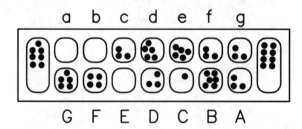

Cup "C" was originally empty, but this does not matter. It is what is held in cup "B" that determines your next move. Since cup "B" contains several stones, you continue playing. Take the stones from cup "B" but none from cup "C", and sow them in the same direction as before, starting with cup "A". The stones on the board are now arranged like this.

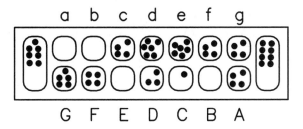

A next-cup continued play does not end until the last stone sown lands in a cup followed by an empty cup. As shown in the figure above, the last stone landed in cup "c", and cup "b" following it was empty, so the next-cup continued play ended.

When the last stone you sow lands in any cup followed by an empty cup, your turn ends, but you may be able to capture. If the empty cup is in turn followed by a loaded cup, you capture the stones from that third cup. Note that you may capture stones from any cup on either side of the board. Take your captured stones and place them in your reservoir. Your opponent makes the next move. This is called skip-cup capturing and it is illustrated by the following figures.

Assume the game is in progress, and after several turns, you see that you can make a capture. You start your next play from cup "F". Before you make your play, the board looks like this.

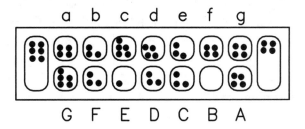

Your last stone sown lands in cup "C", which is followed by an empty cup, cup "B", so your turn ends. Since the cup following "B", cup "A", is loaded, however, you can make a capture. The board now looks like this.

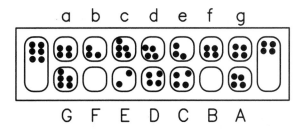

You take the stones from cup "A" (but none from cup "C") and place them in your reservoir. The board now looks like this.

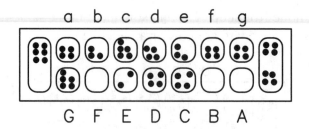

Your opponent makes the next play.

Ending:

The game ends when both sides of the board go empty. The player who has captured more stones wins. If one player's side goes empty before this happens, he passes until his opponent plays something to his side. The opponent must do so at her first opportunity.

Sometimes a game will reach a stalemate where no more captures are possible and to continue playing would be pointless. In this instance, players may agree to end the game and keep any stones remaining on their side.

Variations:

Add capturing of passing-fours

In Pallanguli, any time you sow a stone other than your last into a cup that held three stones, making its total four, the cup becomes a passing-four. Passing-fours may be captured but not necessarily by the player who is sowing. Instead, the player who owns the cup captures them. This means at any time during the game, if a passing-four forms on your side of the board, you capture it. If a passing-four forms on your opponent's side, she captures it. Capturing of passing-fours is illustrated below.

Assume the game is in progress, and you decide to start your next play from cup "D", which holds enough stones to sow through cup "f". Before you make your play, the board looks like this.

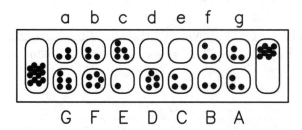

You pick up and sow the stones from cup "D". You pause at cup "A", because it originally held three stones and now holds four, becoming a passing-four. This is shown in the figure below.

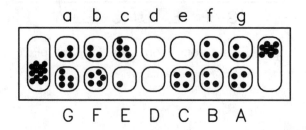

Since cup "A" is on your side of the board, you capture the passing-four. Take the stones and place them in your reservoir. The board now looks like this.

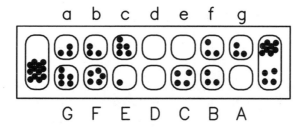

You resume sowing, starting with cup "g", leaving "A" empty. Cup "g" also originally held three stones and now holds four. Thus, it, too, becomes a passing-four as shown in the figure below.

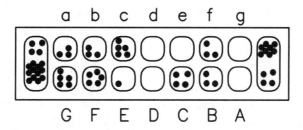

Since cup "g" is on your opponent's side, however, the four stones go to her. She takes them and places them in her reservoir. The board now looks like this.

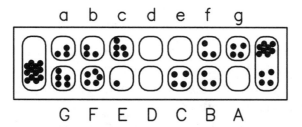

You have one remaining stone, which you sow into cup "f". Cup "f" now holds four stones, as seen in the figure below.

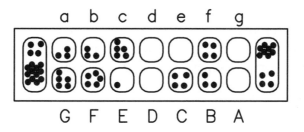

However, since it was the last stone you sowed, "f" does not become a passing-four and the stones remain on the board. Since both cups "e" and "d", following cup "f", are empty, your turn ends and your opponent makes the next play.

A restriction on passing-fours is that you must take the stones immediately. Once the player stops sowing or when a fifth stone is sown into the passing-four, the stones are no longer available for capture. Some players have an additional rule that you must take the stones before a stone is sown into the cup following the passing-four.

After you capture, take another turn

After you capture, if one of the two cups following the one you captured is loaded, you may continue sowing. Start with the cup closer to the one you originally captured. This is a traditional play in Pallanguli. As usual with capture go-again plays, though, we found it gives one player too much of an advantage.

Notes on Strategy:

We found that passing-fours not only add an extra means of capture to Pallanguli, they speed up the game. This is especially the case at the beginning when there are many stones on the board. However, we also felt this feature took some of the challenge out of the game, making it more a game of luck.

PALLANGULI ROUNDS
A Traditional Indian Form

Pallanguli is traditionally played in rounds. The object of any one round is to capture as many stones as possible in order to have as many active cups during the next round as possible. The ultimate goal over a series of rounds is to leave your opponent unable to play, because she has nothing but inactive cups, also called **rubbish holes**.

Eighty-four stones are required. Place six stones in each of the fourteen cups, leaving the two reservoirs empty. For the first round, play as described under One-round Pallanguli, except start the game with six stones per cup instead of four. For the second round, take the stones you captured during the first round and place six in as many of your seven cups as you can. Start with your rightmost cup, nearest your reservoir, and move left. If you can only partially fill a cup, leave it empty for this round and return the extra stones to your reservoir. If you fill all your cups, return any remaining stones to your reservoir.

Any cups you can not fill or can only partially fill become rubbish holes. They will remain empty during this round and will not be used by either player. Place a large stone or similar object in them as a reminder. Start the round with the player whose turn was second on the last round. Play as you did for round one, trying to win enough stones in order to have as few rubbish holes as possible during the next round.

For the third and subsequent rounds, place the stones held in your reservoir back into the cups as described above for round two. Rubbish holes from the previous round can become active again if enough stones were captured in the previous round. Start each new round with the person who started second in the last round.

Rounds continue until one player has fewer than six stones, leaving her nothing on the board but rubbish holes. However, once one player is down to three or fewer cups, a point at which it is almost impossible to recover, players usually agree to end the game. The player who has more active cups wins.

Variations: Pallanguli Rounds may be and typically is played with the variations under One-round Pallanguli.

PANDI
Pallanguli with Bonus Capture

Pandi is a variation of Pallanguli that is played in southern India. It is played like Pallanguli Rounds with the following exceptions. First, the game starts with five stones per cup instead of six. This allows for a faster game. Second, whenever you make a regular capture (not a passing-four capture), you may additionally take the stones held in the cup directly across from it on the opposite side of the board, called a bonus capture.

The passing-fours variation discussed under One-round Pallanguli may also be included in Pandi. However, we found that allowing two forms of secondary capture resulted in an unbalanced game.

LONGBEU-A-CHA
Pallanguli with Alternating Series Capture

Longbeu-a-cha is a variation of Pallanguli played by the Lakhar people of Assam, a state in northeastern India. It is played like Pallanguli Rounds, except for the following differences. First, Longbeu-a-cha starts with five stones per cup. Second, in addition to passing-fours it allows another form of secondary capture, the alternating series capture.

Similar to series capturing in Wari, the alternating series capture allows you to capture stones from a series of cups on a single play. However, in the alternating series capture, the extra cups must follow rather than precede the cup you originally captured. In addition, the series is not restricted to just one side of the board. It may continue onto the other side.

The series must consist of alternating empty and loaded cups, and the first cup of the series (the one immediately following the cup you originally captured) must be empty. You capture stones held in any cup in the series, plus, of course, the cup you originally captured. Take the stones and place them in your reservoir. The alternating cup capture is illustrated below.

Assume the game is in progress, and you start your next play from cup "F". Before you make your play, the board looks like this.

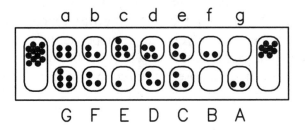

Your last stone sown lands in cup "C", and the board looks like this.

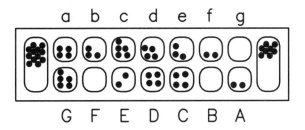

Since cup "C" is followed by an empty cup, cup "B", and then a loaded one, cup "A", you capture the stones in cup "A". Additionally, since cup "A" is followed by an empty cup, cup "g", that is in turn followed by a loaded cup, cup "f", you also capture the stones in cup "f". Take your captured stones and place them in your reservoir. The board now looks like this.

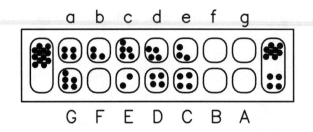

Since cup "e" is loaded, the alternating pattern breaks down and no further captures are possible. Your turn ends and your opponent takes the next turn.

Notes on Strategy:

At first glance, the alternating series capture may seem like a very generous form of secondary capture, because theoretically you can use it to clear the entire board on one play. However, it is more difficult to accomplish than it seems. For one thing, the pattern of alternating empty and loaded cups is hard to set up, especially on your opponent's side of the board where you have little control. In addition, since this game has continued play, the stones are constantly being mixed. It can be difficult to set up a long alternating series, especially earlier in the game when there are many stones on the board. Despite its limitations, though, alternating series capture adds some challenge to Pallanguli, decreasing the dependence of winning on luck.

OLINDA
Pallanguli Played in Opposite Directions

Olinda is a variation of Pallanguli that is played in Sri Lanka. It is played like One-round Pallanguli with any variation, except for the following differences. First, Olinda starts with five stones per cup rather than six. Second, players play in opposite directions. Note, however, that your reservoir always remains on your right, no matter what direction you are sowing.

The player who goes first chooses a direction of play. He may sow clockwise or counterclockwise, as suits his strategy. His opponent must then play in the opposite direction. Once the direction of play is established, it remains unchanged for the entire game.

Playing in Rounds:

Olinda may be played in rounds using the rules for Pallanguli Rounds. At the beginning of a new round, the player who went second on the previous round goes first. However, this time she chooses the direction of play, and the other player must play in the opposite direction.

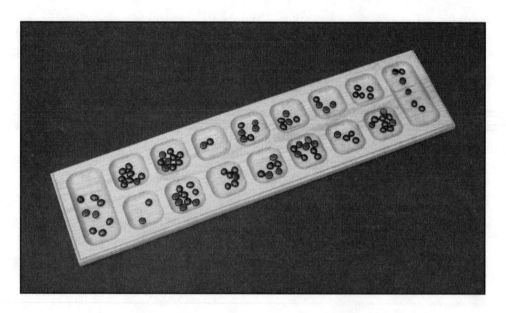

**Filipino Sungka board with seven cups per row made by
authors.**

SUNGKA: SOUTHEAST ASIAN MANCALA

SUNGKA, ALSO KNOWN as Sunca, Dakon, Chonka, Chongkak, Jongkak, and Chunkajohn, is the traditional form of mancala played in the Philippines and other parts of Southeast Asia. It is played similarly to an American version called Cross Capture Mancala and may even be its parent game. However, Sungka has a number of features that make it different. For one thing, it is played on a longer board with more stones. In addition, it is played in rounds where players gain and lose cups from round to round according to how many stones they captured at the end of the previous round. What really makes Sungka different, though, is that for the first play of the first round, players play simultaneously. This is a feature found in few other versions of mancala.

There is little information on the origins of mancala games played in the Philippines and Southeast Asia. However, it is possible that mancala itself was introduced from India. Sungka has many features in common with the Indian version of Pallanguli. Both games are played on boards with seven cups per row and start with the less common five to seven stones per cup. Also, both are played in rounds and have the same ultimate goal of leaving the opponent unable to play because she has nothing but inactive cups.

Sungka has some interesting characteristics. It is an unusually lengthy game and between players of equal ability, it has been known to go on for days. In addition, among some players, cheating is part of the game. If a player can palm a few extra stones to finish his play or add to his reservoir, it is acceptable as long as he is not caught. (We have often wondered what happens to a player if he *is* caught.)

Sungka is also interesting culturally. In the Philippines, Sungka is traditionally played only at wakes to amuse the spirits of the deceased until they depart for the next world. The game must be put away at sundown, however, and it must not be stored in the house. If it is, it will bring bad luck to the owners, or worse, the dead will come back to play. From the number of Filipino players we have met who are avid Sungka players, though, it appears unlikely that this superstition is taken very seriously. Of course, there are always exceptions. One Filipino player told us that his grandmother let no one play Sungka in the house for fear it would bring the family bad luck. Finally in a moment of panic, she burned the board. Sadly, it had been in the family for generations.

There do not appear to be many variations of Sungka. Like Pallanguli, names abound, but the games are played by nearly the same rules. So again, we have combined the instructions for similar variations under one basic heading as we did for Pallanguli. We did encounter one variation of Sungka that was different enough to be placed under a separate heading, however. It is called Jongkak and is played in Malaysia.

ONE-ROUND SUNGKA
The Basic Game

Sungka is among the more advanced mancala games there are and can be difficult to master, especially if you are new to mancala. So, included here is a simplified version called One-round

Sungka. It teaches the basics of traditional or Burnt House Sungka while eliminating some of the more confusing rules, such as playing simultaneously.

While we have not encountered many written variations of Sungka, we have been taught a few by Filipino players we have met through Happy Viking. Included below, these variations do not significantly change the game, but they do add an interesting twist to it.

Object: To capture more stones than your opponent by the end of the game.

Gameboard: The gameboard consists of two rows of seven cups and a reservoir at each end for storing stones captured during the game. Players each own half the cups. Your cups would be cups "A" through "G" and your opponent's cups, "a" through "g" as shown below. Since stones are sown through your reservoir, reservoirs are owned. You own the reservoir on your right.

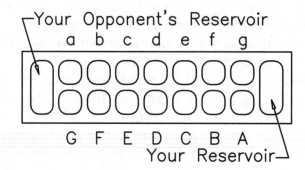

Board Setup: Ninety-eight stones are required. Place seven stones in each of the fourteen cups, leaving the two reservoirs empty.

Playing:

Randomly choose a player to start. To make a play, take all the stones from any one of your seven cups and sow them all counterclockwise around the board. Sow one stone per cup starting with the cup next to the one from which you originally took the stones. You may sow through all fourteen cups plus your reservoir but not your opponent's reservoir. All stones that land in your reservoir are yours and remain there until the end of the game.

If the last stone you sow lands in a cup on either side of the board that already contains one or more stones, continue playing. Take the stones from that cup and sow them as described above, starting with the next cup. Continue sowing in this manner until your last stone lands in your reservoir or an empty cup. The figures below illustrate this play, called a continued play.

Assume the game is in progress, and you are about to make your next play. The board looks like this.

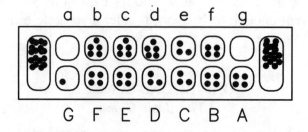

You take all the stones from cup "B" and sow them counterclockwise. The last stone sown lands in cup "f" and the board now looks like this.

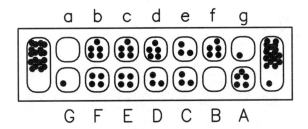

Since cup "f" was loaded, you continue playing. You pick up the stones in cup "f", including the last stone sown. Then you sow them in the same direction as before, starting with cup "e". The stones on the board are now arranged like this.

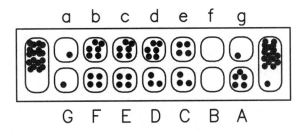

A continued play ends when the last stone sown lands in an empty cup or your reservoir. As shown in the figure above, the last stone sown landed in cup "a", which was previously empty, and the continued play ended.

If the last stone you sow lands in your reservoir, you may make another play. Take all the stones from any one cup on your side of the board and sow them as described above. If the last stone lands in an empty cup your turn ends, but you may be able to cross capture. If the empty cup is on your side of the board, and the cup across from it on your opponent's side is loaded, take those stones plus your last stone sown and place them in your reservoir. Your opponent makes the next play. Cross capturing, as used in Sungka, is shown in the following figures.

Assume the game is in progress, and you see that you can capture some of your opponent's stones. Before you make your play, the board looks like this.

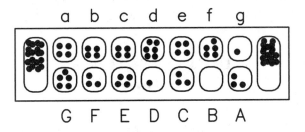

You start your play from cup "G", and your last stone sown lands in cup "B", which is empty, but it is across from cup "f", which contains several stones. The board now looks like this.

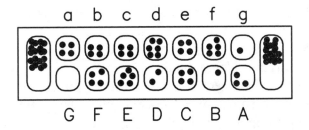

97

You take the stones from cup "f" plus your last stone sown (in cup "B") and place them in your reservoir. The board now looks like this.

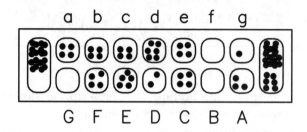

Ending:

The game ends when you make a play and all six cups on your side of the board become empty. You capture all the stones remaining in your opponent's cups. Move these stones to your reservoir. The winner is the player who has more stones in his reservoir.

Variations:

Add rightmost cup capture

Play as instructed above, except for the following change. When your last stone sown lands in your reservoir, you capture any stones in your rightmost cup, cup "A" next to your reservoir. You may then take another turn. (Some players do not allow the extra turn.)

Change your reservoir to the one on the left

Play as instructed above, except use the reservoir on your left instead of your right. However, do not change the direction of play. Continue to sow your stones counterclockwise around the board as before. This may sound like a trivial change, but you will be surprised how much it affects the game.

End when both sides of the board go empty

The game ends when both sides of the board go empty. If one player's side goes empty before this happens, he passes until his opponent plays something to his side. The opponent must do so at the first opportunity. The player with more captured stones at the end of the game wins.

BURNT HOUSE SUNGKA
A Traditional Filipino Form

Burnt House Sungka is the traditional form of Sungka played in Southeast Asia. It is played like One-round Sungka and any of the variations may be used. (Burnt House Sungka also has a variation of its own.) The differences are that Burnt House Sungka begins differently, and it is played in rounds.

Before beginning, it is helpful to know some of the Sungka terminology, which is used in the instructions below. The cups on the gameboard are referred to as your **houses** and your reservoir is a **storehouse**. Houses that become inactive during a round are called **burnt houses**, thus the name Burnt House Sungka. When a player can no longer play because his last stone has landed in an empty cup, he has **died** or is considered **dead**.

In Burnt House Sungka, the object of any one round is to capture as many stones as possible in order to have as many active cups during the next round as possible. The ultimate goal over a series of rounds is to leave your opponent unable to play because she has nothing but burnt houses.

Ninety-eight stones are required. For the first round, place seven stones in each of the fourteen houses, leaving the two storehouses empty. For subsequent rounds, set up the board as directed below. Note: for a faster game, start with five or six stones per cup instead of seven.

For the opening play of the first round, do not choose a player to begin, because both players will play simultaneously. To play simultaneously, you start your plays and sow as for any alternating play. The only difference is that you and your opponent will do this at the same time.

When playing simultaneously, you may pass your opponent if you like. In addition, if you have an opportunity to cross capture, you may do so, although it will end your play. If there is a dispute over some stones - for instance, you capture some stones just as your opponent is about to pick up those same stones and sow them - the one to grab them first gets them.

The first play of the first round is the one and only where you will play simultaneously. From the second play on and throughout the rest of the game, players will alternate turns. The player who dies first on the simultaneous play will make the first alternating play. From this point on, you will play as for One-round Sungka.

For the second round, take the stones from your reservoir and place seven in each of your cups, starting with your rightmost cup, cup "A" next to your reservoir, and moving left. If you fill all your cups, return any remaining stones to your reservoir. If you can only partially fill a cup, leave it empty for this round and return the extra stones to your reservoir.

Any cups that are empty, because you can not fill them or can only partially fill them, are burnt houses. They will remain empty and will not be used by either player during this round. Place a marker in each burnt house as a reminder. (Native players do not allow markers. Instead, you must memorize where the burnt houses are.) If you inadvertently sow a stone into your opponent's burnt house, your opponent automatically captures the stone.

Start the new round with the player who won the previous round. That would be the player who holds more stones. (Note: some players start subsequent rounds with the player who lost the last round. This results in a lengthier game but gives the loser a better chance of winning back some of her burnt houses.) Play as directed in One-round Sungka. As you play, try to win enough stones to make any burnt houses you may have active again.

A new round begins with the stones in each reservoir being placed back in the cups as described above. Repeat rounds until one player has fewer than seven stones. This leaves her unable to fill any cups and therefore she loses, because she has nothing left but burnt houses.

Variations:

Choose the cups you refill at the start of a new round

Play as instructed above, except for the following change. When starting a new round, if you do not have enough stones to fill all of your cups, you may choose the cups you fill. As before, place any remaining stones back into your reservoir.

Comments:

It is easy to misunderstand the simultaneous play. For instance, some players have thought you play simultaneously for the first play of each round. Others have thought you play simultaneously throughout the game. Of course, both these variations add an interesting element to the game, and you are welcome to try them if you like. However, in traditional Sungka, you only play simultaneously for the first play of the first round.

Notes on Strategy:

Sungka can be tricky, so here are some pointers. To begin with, since playing simultaneously is seldom used in American mancala games, it may initially seem of little value other than determining who goes first. However, it can strategically be a very important play. The trick is to use the simultaneous play to give yourself an advantage over your opponent.

To do this, sow as fast as you can, capturing as many stones as you can. Passing your opponent is desirable, because it gives you more control of the board. Second, keep sowing as long as you can. Your opponent has a real opportunity to get ahead once you die. Understandably, it is difficult to control this, but you can do several things. Since you choose the cup you start from, you can avoid any that are obvious dead ends. Also, you can speed up or slow down your sowing, allowing your opponent to feed a stone into an empty cup that would otherwise end your play. In the event you do die first, check to see if you can make a cross capture, but be fast. Your opponent can take your captured stones if it is part of her legal play and she gets to them first.

A second point of strategy is keeping as many cups active from round to round as possible. If even one cup becomes inactive at the end of a round, you are at a disadvantage. Not only do you have one fewer cup to start plays from, but also the cup across from it on your opponent's side becomes immune to cross capture. She can use that cup to hoard stones for a strategic play. This situation gets worse as more of your cups become inactive.

Fortunately, you can still recover if you only have one or two inactive cups, but it becomes increasingly difficult to capture enough stones beyond that, since so many of them are in your opponent's reservoir. Obviously, the key to avoiding this situation is to capture as many stones as you can during any round. This means relying more heavily on cross capturing and less on stones you sow into your reservoir. Of course, a cross capture may take several turns to set up and you may have to sacrifice a chance to feed your reservoir, but in the long run you will come out better.

Some final points, do not give your opponent capturing opportunities by letting too many stones build up in one cup, unless the cup is safe from attack. In addition, if you are playing the game using a go-empty ending, by going empty at the right time, you can make a substantial capture.

JONGKAK
A Malaysian Form of Sungka

Jongkak is a variation of Sungka played in Malaysia. According to local legend, only the ladies of the royal court originally played it. Nowadays, though, anyone may play. Like Sungka, Jongkak has some interesting terminology that is used when referring to the game. The name Jongkak refers to the shape of the board, a *jong* or junk in English. The cups on your side of the board are known as your **village**. Your reservoir is your **house**. When you make a capture, the stones **enter your house**. At the start of a new round, any cups that become inactive are called **ruined wells**. If you land in an empty cup, you are said to be **dead**. Finally, if you lose a round, you are **once defeated**, but if you lose the match, you are **utterly destroyed**.

Jongkak is played like Burnt House Sungka, except for the following changes. The game still ends when it is your opponent's turn and she can no longer play because her side of the board is empty. You capture all the stones that remain on your side, but you do not move them to your reservoir. Instead, you leave them where they are. Only your opponent reloads her cups, using what she has stored in her reservoir.

For example, assume a round ends because your opponent went empty. As in Burnt House Sungka, she takes the stones from her reservoir and fills as many of her cups as she can with seven stones, starting with her rightmost cup "a" and moving left. (You may alternately let players choose the cups they reload.) Any unfilled or partially filled cups become inactive and she returns any leftover stones to her reservoir.

Meanwhile, the stones in your cups and reservoir are left where they were when the last round ended. This means the number of stones held in your cups remains unchanged, as does the status of your cups. Therefore, if they were inactive during the last round, they stay inactive. The new round then begins and you make the first play.

Notes on Strategy:

Because one, rather than both players, reloads his cups before starting a new round, you must avoid going empty. The reason is when you go empty, the stones in your reservoir are re-entered onto the board. They become available to your opponent for capture, while hers remain safe in her reservoir. However, a difficulty that she may encounter if you go empty first is that if she has any inactive cups, they will remain so for the next round. You, on the other hand, may be able to reactivate inactive cups.

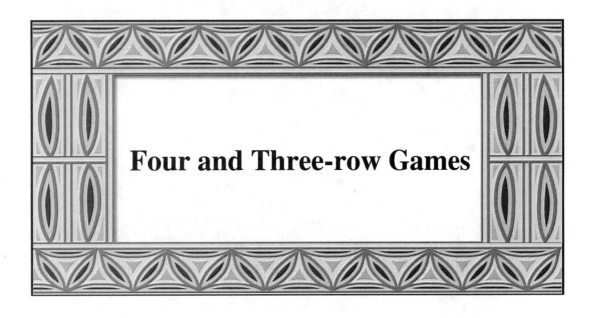

Four and Three-row Games

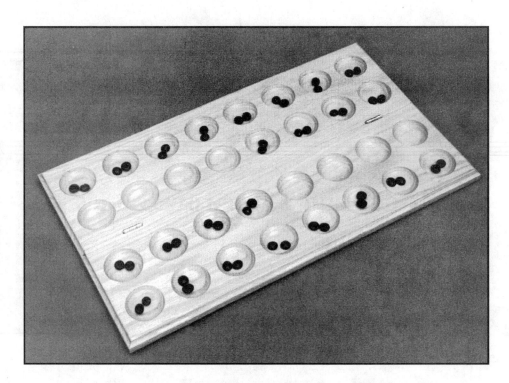

Four-row mancala board made by authors.

FOUR-ROW MANCALA

FOUR-ROW MANCALA is played in eastern and southern Africa, being almost exclusive to this area. Although definitely mancala, it differs from two-row mancala in a number of ways. The most obvious difference is the gameboard, which has four rows of cups rather than two. Players still each own half the cups on the board, but they own two rows of cups instead of just one. In addition, the path of play is different. In four-row games, players sow only through their two rows, never crossing to the opponent's side.

Another difference between two-row and four-row games is that while most two-row games are capture games, four-row games are almost without exception disable games. That is, the object is not to capture more stones than your opponent. It is to disable your opponent either by capturing all of her stones or enough of them to leave her unable to play. The result is four-row games play quite differently from their two-row cousins.

Regarding the origins of four-row mancala, several theories exist. One maintains that the Arabs introduced this version of mancala to Africa. The four-row game of Kiarabu played in Zanzibar literally translates to "the Arab game". However, another theory claims that four-row mancala developed in Africa. Evidence to support this is the number of variations played there. In addition, until recently four-row mancala has never been played elsewhere.

While no one can be certain where four-row mancala originated, it clearly has been played for many centuries. During excavations of mines in Zimbabwe, remnants of several stone, four-row gameboards have been found. These mines are near a civilization that existed in Zimbabwe and Rhodesia from 1400 to 1850 AD.

Today there are hundreds of four-row games played throughout Africa. Included in this chapter are several of the more typical ones. They are organized into two sections, according to the type of capture used. The first section includes cross capture games. They are the best games to start with if you are new to four-row mancala. The second section includes pull-across capture games. They are more typical of four-row games but also more difficult to learn.

One note on gameboards: the number of the cups per row in four-row games varies considerably, even for the same game. However, we found eight cups per row provides a good balance between challenge and a convenient size. Thus, all games in this chapter have been adapted accordingly.

CROSS CAPTURE GAMES

MEFUHVA
The Basic Game

Mefuhva is played in northern Transvaal, a province in the northeastern part of the Republic of South Africa. It is one of the easiest four-row games to play, because neither the rules nor the strategy is overly complicated.

Mefuhva is culturally interesting. For one thing, although players generally use seeds for playing pieces, during the rainy season they will not. They fear doing so might cause severe thunderstorms. In addition, the number of cups per row used in Mefuhva varies more than most four-row games. While sixteen is typical, boards with six, eight, and twelve cups per row are also quite common. There are even boards with twenty-eight cups per row, possibly the longest gameboard used in mancala.

Object: To clear your opponent's side of the board by capturing all of her stones.

Gameboard: The gameboard has four rows of cups with eight cups per row. Cups are divided equally among players and they each "own" the half on the side of the board that they face. For you, these would be cups "A" through "P", for your opponent, cups "a" through "p" as shown in the figure below.

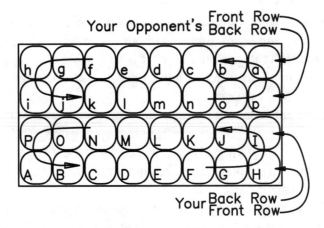

Since there is no need to keep a count of captured stones, reservoirs are not included on most four-row gameboards.

Board Setup: Fifty-eight stones are required. Leave the leftmost cup in your front row empty and place one stone in the cup directly to its right. Then place two stones in each of the remaining cups as shown below.

Alternative Setup: We found that the traditional setup made capturing too easy for the first player. A setup where all cups started with two stones seemed to work better. This requires sixty-four stones total.

Playing:

Randomly choose a player to start. To make a play, take all the stones from any one of your cups that contain two or more stones. Although, you may start a play from a cup containing a singleton, this is only if no other plays are possible and only if you can sow that stone into an empty cup.

Sow the stones counterclockwise through your two rows only. Do not sow through your opponent's two rows. (Refer to the figure shown under **Gameboard** for an illustration of the path of play.) Sow one stone per cup, starting with the cup next to the one from which you originally took the stones. Leave the cup you took the stones from empty.

If your last stone sown lands in a loaded cup in either of your two rows, continue playing. Take the stones from that cup and sow them through your two rows as before, again starting with the next cup. Continue sowing in this manner until the last stone sown lands in an empty cup. The figures below illustrate this play, called a continued play.

Assume the game is in progress and you are about to take your next turn. Before you play, the board looks like this.

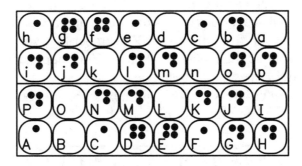

You take all the stones from cup "K" and sow them counterclockwise. The last stone sown lands in cup "N", and the board now looks like this.

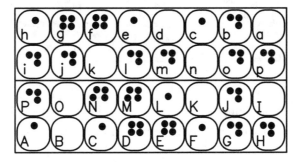

Since cup "N" already held three stones and now holds four, you continue playing. You pick up all four stones in cup "N" and, leaving it empty, sow them in the same direction. The stones on the board are now arranged like this.

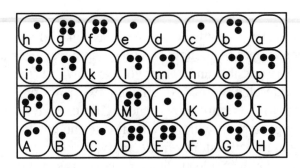

The continued play does not end until the last stone sown lands in an empty cup. As shown in the figure above, the last stone sown landed in cup "B", which was previously empty, so the continued play ended.

Landing in an empty cup always ends your turn. However, you may be able to cross capture. If the empty cup is in your front row and the cup across from it in your opponent's front row contains one or more stones, you capture those stones but not your last stone sown. If there are also stones in your opponent's adjacent back row cup, you capture those as well. Take all of your captured stones and remove them from the board. Remember that you do not need to keep track of captured stones, so where you put them does not matter. Your opponent makes the next play. Cross capturing as used in four-row games is illustrated below.

Assume the game is in progress and on your next turn you see that you can capture some of your opponent's stones. Before you start your play, the board looks like this.

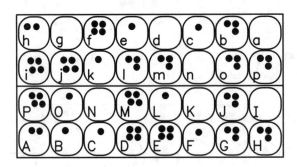

You pick up the stones from cup "E" and sow them counterclockwise. The last stone sown lands in cup "I" in your front row. Since cup "I" is empty and cup "p" directly across from it holds three stones, you capture the three stones. Remove them from the board. If cup "a" behind cup "p" were also loaded, you would capture and remove those stones as well. However, you do not capture your last stone sown which remains in cup "I". After removing your captured stones, the board looks like this.

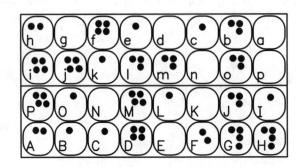

Ending:

The game ends and you win when your opponent is unable to make anymore plays, because her side of the board is empty of all stones. The number of stones captured by each player is not important.

CHISOLO
Choose Your Direction of Play

Chisolo is an intermediate game played by the Ba-ila speaking people of northern Rhodesia. It is played like Mefuhva, except that it starts with three stones in each cup. In addition, before you take your second turn, you must choose your direction of play, either clockwise or counterclockwise. You will play in your chosen direction for the rest of the game. Your opponent does likewise before her second turn. Note that you and your opponent may end up playing in opposite directions.

Notes on Strategy:

Chisolo is a game of attrition that moves quickly, especially at the beginning when big captures are easy to make. You may be misled into thinking it is therefore an easy game. However, as there are fewer and fewer stones on the board, capturing becomes harder. When players are down to their last stones it takes clever maneuvering to capture without being captured.

TSORO
Add Headers

Tsoro is an intermediate game played in Zimbabwe. It is played like Mefuhva but starts with two stones in each cup. In addition, before beginning the game, you and your opponent must choose two cups from your back row to be your headers. (Front row cups can not be headers.)

Players are not required to choose the same headers, although they often do. Cups typically chosen are either

- The two leftmost back row cups ("A" and "B" for you, "a" and "b" for your opponent)
- The leftmost and rightmost back row cups ("A" and "H" for you, "a" and "h" for your opponent)

In the latter case, players often start the game with three stones per cup instead of two.

Headers are restricted cups. You may start a play from a header or sow through it. However, stones held in them may not be captured. So, if you capture a cup in your opponent's front row and the loaded cup directly behind it is a header, you only capture the stones held in the front row cup. The stones held in the header stay where they are. However, remember your opponent may not capture your headers either. Thus, in this sense headers are also safe cups.

Headers allow you special privileges. If the last stone you sow lands in one of your headers and it is loaded, you have a choice of actions. You may continue playing as you usually would or you may end your play. By doing the latter, you can control the number of stones held in the header and can use it later for a strategic move.

Variations:

<u>Choose your bonus cup</u>

If you capture a cup in your opponent's front row and there is a loaded cup directly behind it that is not a header, you have two choices of action. You may take the stones from the back row cup as you normally would. Alternatively, you may take the stones from a different cup in her back row, as long as it is not a header.

Comments:

Some players allow taking two or three back row cups on a capture, agreeing on the number before beginning the game. However, we found this greatly reduced the challenge of the game and recommend taking only one bonus cup.

PULL-ACROSS CAPTURE GAMES

HUS
The Basic Game

Hus is a four-row version of mancala played by the Hottentot people of southern Africa. Among pull-across capture games, it is one of the easier ones to play, since its rules are not overly complicated. The strategy is not quite as straightforward as the cross capture games, however. Since players capture stones back and forth rather than removing them from the board, getting ahead can be difficult, especially between equally matched players. This is because the more stones one player gets on his side, the more vulnerable he is to capture. The opponent can easily capture them back to her side if she has planned carefully and not fallen too far behind. Therefore, Hus can turn around several times before a winner emerges.

Object: To clear your opponent's side of the board either by capturing all of her stones to your side or enough of them so she has stones but none she can play.

Gameboard: The gameboard consists of four rows of cups with eight cups per row. Cups are divided equally among players and they each "own" the half on the side of the board that they face.

Board Setup: Forty-eight stones are required. Place two stones in each cup except the four leftmost cups in your front row, which are left empty. This is shown below.

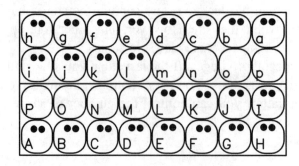

Playing:

Randomly choose a player to start. To make a play, take all the stones from any one of your sixteen cups that contain at least two stones. You may never start a play from a cup containing a singleton. Sow the stones counterclockwise through your two rows only. Do not sow through your opponent's two rows. Sow one stone per cup, starting with the cup next to the one from which you originally took the stones. Leave the cup you originally took the stones from empty.

If the last stone you sow lands in an empty cup in either of your rows, your turn ends. If it lands in your back row in a loaded cup, continue playing. Take the stones from that cup and sow them through your two rows as before, starting with the next cup. If the last stone you sow lands in a loaded cup in your front row and the cup across from it in your opponent's front row is empty, do likewise. Continue sowing in this manner until your last stone sown lands in either an empty cup or a loaded front row cup across from a loaded cup on your opponent's side. (This is the continued play move illustrated in Mefuhva in the last section.)

If the last stone you sow lands in a loaded cup in your front row and the cup across from it in your opponent's front row is loaded, you make a pull-across capture. Take the stones from your opponent's front row cup plus any in the cup directly behind it but none from the cup where your last stone was sown. However, rather than removing the captured stones from the board, sow them onto your side. Sow through your two rows, starting with the cup following the one where your last stone landed when you made the capture. The pull-across capture used in Hus is illustrated below.

Assume the game is in progress and after several turns, you see that you can capture some of your opponent's stones to your side. Before you make your play, the board looks like this.

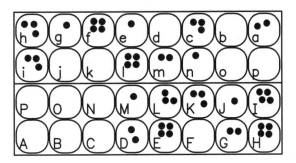

You start your next play from cup "I" and your last stone sown lands in cup "M", a loaded cup in your front row. The board now looks like this.

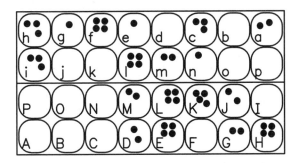

Since cup "l" on your opponent's side (across from cup "M") is also loaded, you make a capture. You take the stones from cup "l", plus any stones in cup "e" directly behind it, but none from cup "M". You then sow those stones onto your side, starting with cup "N". The board now looks like this.

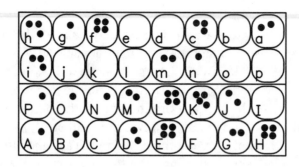

Continue sowing and capturing in this manner, until your last stone sown lands in an empty cup in either row. This ends your turn and your opponent makes the next play. There is no limit on the number of captures allowed on one turn.

Ending:

The game ends and you win when your opponent is unable to make anymore plays, because she has only singletons left or her side of the board is empty of all stones. The latter case is more difficult to accomplish and therefore counts as a double win. The number of stones captured by each player is not important.

Playing in Rounds:

Hus is traditionally played in rounds. For the first round, randomly choose a player to start and play as directed above. For subsequent rounds, the player who won the previous round starts the new round. At the end of the game, score one point for each game won, adding a bonus point if you made a double win. The player with more points at the end of seven rounds is the winner.

BARE'
Add Simultaneous Play, Modify Capturing

Bare' is a game played by the Anuak people of western Ethiopia. Play as instructed in Hus, except for the following changes. First, sixty-four stones are needed. Start the game with two stones in each cup. Next, do not choose a player to begin. For the opening play, you and your opponent will play simultaneously. This play occurs once at the beginning of the game. After it is completed, the game returns to regular alternating play.

When playing simultaneously, play by the same rules you would for playing alternately. This means that you start your play, sow, and capture as for any alternating play. If there is a dispute over some captured stones, the one to grab them first gets them. Once the simultaneous play ends, the player who ended first makes the first alternating play.

Capturing is a little different in Bare'. To capture, the last stone you sow must still land in a loaded cup in your front row. However, both cups across from it (in your opponent's front and back rows) must be loaded. Take the stones from these cups but none from the cup where your last stone was sown. Rather than removing them from the board, though, sow the captured stones onto your side as you did in Hus. Note: in Bare', if you miss an opportunity to capture, your opponent may move the stones from one of the two threatened cups to the other as a hedge against future capture.

Comments:

As far as we can tell, simultaneous play seldom appears in African mancala games, being almost exclusive to the games of Southeast Asia. How it came to be used in Bare' is not clear. It would be interesting to know if this play is more commonly used in African mancala than has been documented.

Playing in Rounds: Bare' may be played in rounds using the rules given for Hus.

OMWESO
Add Backup Pull-across Capture

Omweso is played by the Baganda people of Uganda. It is played like Bare', except for the following differences. First, sixty-four stones are required. Place four stones in each back row cup, leaving the front row cups empty. The setup is shown below.

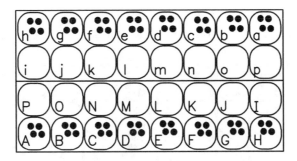

Second, there is no simultaneous play, although you may use it if you like.

Finally, while Omweso has standard pull-across capture, it additionally allows a variation of this called a backup pull-across capture or simply **backup capture**. In a backup capture, your last stone sown must still land in a loaded cup in your front row that is across from two loaded cups on your opponent's side. The difference is that you are allowed to reverse your direction of play from counterclockwise (the usual direction of play) to clockwise in order to make the backup capture. However, there are restrictions on when and how you may do this.

First, while you may make a backup capture on either a new play or a continued play, that play must start or continue from one of your two leftmost cups in either row. For you this would be cups "A", "B", "O", and "P", and for your opponent, cups "a", "b", "o", and "p", as seen in the figure below.

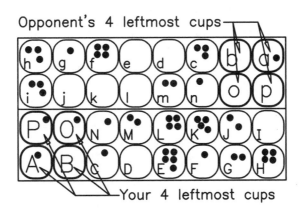

Second, the cup you start or continue your play from may contain no more than nine stones. In the case of the continued play, that includes your last stone sown. The following figures illustrate the backup capture.

Assume that the game is in progress, and you see that by starting from cup "P" you can make a backup capture. Before you make your play, the board looks like this.

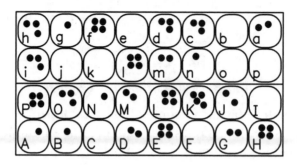

You pick up the stones from cup "P" and sow them backward (clockwise). Your last stone sown lands in cup "L", a loaded cup in your front row. The board now looks like this.

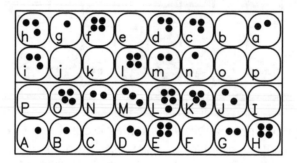

Since both "m" and "d" across form "L" are loaded, you capture the stones held in those cups but none from cup "L". You take the captured stones, but do not sow them just yet. The board now looks like this with the five stones you captured from cups "m" and "d" still in your hand.

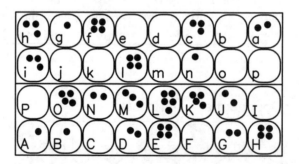

Once you complete a backup capture, you have two options. Your first option is to make a second backup capture if one is possible. This will be explained momentarily. Your second option, and the one you must choose if you can not make a second backup capture, is to take your captured stones and resume sowing forward (counterclockwise). However, you do not start with the cup following the one where your last stone landed when you captured. Instead, you start with the cup following the one from which you started your backup capture.

Continuing the previous example, assume you consider the second option. This means that you would resume sowing forward (counterclockwise) from cup "A", because you started your backup capture from cup "P". Your last stone sown would then land in cup "E" as shown below.

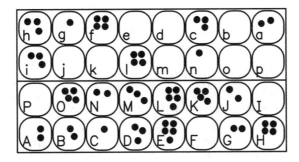

Since cup "E" was originally loaded, the play would continue by you taking the stones from cup "E" and sowing them counterclockwise around the board.

The first option, making a second backup capture, may be more desirable. However, you must meet several criteria. First, the stones captured during your previous backup capture must not exceed nine. Second, your backup capture must start from the cup preceding the one from which you started your previous backup capture. This cup must again be one of your two leftmost cups in either row, "A", "B", "O", and "P" for you and "a", "b", "o", and "p" for your opponent.

Continuing the example above, (but starting two figures back) you see that you meet the criteria for a second backup capture. Since it would be more advantageous to you than resuming sowing forward, you choose this option. You take your captured stones (which are still in your hand) and sow them backward (clockwise), starting from cup "O". Again, you start from this cup, because it is the one preceding the cup where you started your first backup capture. Once you finish sowing, the last of your captured stones lands in cup "K", and the board looks like this.

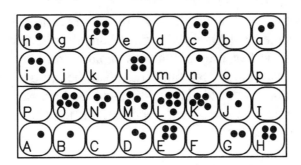

As before, you take your newly captured stones from loaded cups "n" and "c" but none from cup "K" and hold onto them. The board now looks like this.

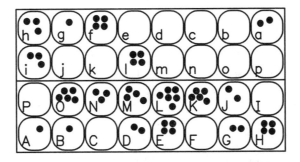

After making a second backup capture, you again have the same two options. However, since your last backup capture started from cup "O", the next one would start from cup "N". This is not allowed, so no more backup captures are possible at this time. Thus, your only option is to

115

resume sowing forward (counterclockwise), the second option discussed above. Since your last backup capture started from cup "O", you must resume sowing from cup "P". After you sow the stones, the board looks like this.

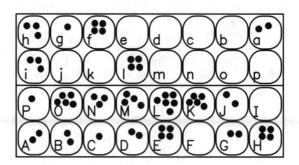

Once you resume sowing counterclockwise, sow and capture as you did before you made your first backup capture. You may make multiple regular and backup captures during one turn, and up to four backup captures are possible in one series. Continue sowing and capturing until your last stone lands in an empty cup in either row, ending your turn.

Playing in Rounds: Omweso may be played in rounds using the rules given for Hus.

KISOLO
Bare' with a Mankala'h and Pallanguli Influence

Kisolo is played by the Ba-luba people of Zaire, a country in west central Africa. It is played similarly to Bare', but has elements of Mankala'h and Pallanguli (discussed in previous chapters). Like Bare', Kisolo is a disable game that uses pull-across capture and plays may never be started from singletons. Like Mankala'h, players may rearrange the board before beginning the game. Finally, like Pallanguli, Kisolo uses next-cup continued play and next-cup pull-across capture.

The object of the game is to clear your opponent's side of the board either by capturing all of her stones to your side or enough of them so

- She has only singletons remaining
- Stones remain in her back row but no stones remain in her front row

Forty-eight stones are required. Place three stones in each of the eight cups in your back row. Leave your front row cups empty. This is shown in the figure below.

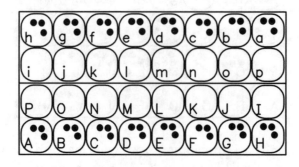

After choosing a player to go first, the other player may rearrange the stones on both sides of the board. If the player to go first is dissatisfied with the setup, he may again rearrange the stones but only on his side. If he does this, however, he forfeits his right to go first.

To make a play, take the stones from any of your cups containing at least two stones. However, in Kisolo it will not be the cup where your last stone lands, but the cup following it that determines your next action. Therefore, if the last stone you sow lands in a cup in either of your rows followed by an empty cup, your turn ends. It does not matter what is held in the cup where your last stone is sown.

If your last stone lands in a cup followed by a loaded cup, however, your turn continues. The action you will take, though, will again depend on the circumstances. If the loaded cup is in your back row, you make a next-cup continued play. Take the stones from the loaded cup and, leaving it empty, sow them as you did before, starting with the next consecutive cup. If the loaded cup is in your front row and <u>either</u> of the cups directly across from it on your opponent's side is empty, do likewise. The figures below illustrate the next-cup continued play as used in Bare'.

Assume the game is in progress and you are about to take your next turn. Before you play, the board looks like this.

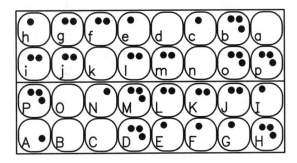

You take all the stones from cup "D" and sow them counterclockwise. The last stone sown lands in cup "G", and the board now looks like this.

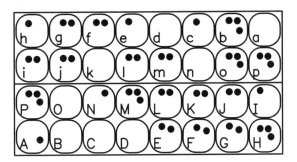

Cup "H", following cup "G", is in your back row and it is loaded, so you continue playing. Take the stones from "H" and, leaving it empty, sow them starting with cup "I". Your last stone sown lands in cup "K". The stones on the board are now arranged like this.

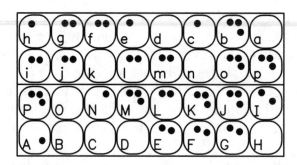

Cup "L", following cup "K", is also loaded. Since it is in your front row and across from at least one empty cup on your opponent's side, in this case cup "m", you again continue playing. Take the stones from cup "L" and sow them, starting with cup "M". Your last stone sown lands in cup "N". The stones on the board are now arranged like this.

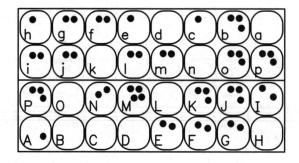

Since cup "O", following cup "N", is empty, your turn ends and your opponent makes the next play.

If your last stone sown lands in a cup in your front row, however, you may be able to capture. If the cup <u>following</u> the one where your last stone landed is loaded, and both cups across from it on your opponent's side are also loaded, you capture. Take the stones from both your opponent's cups but none from your own. However, rather than removing them from the board, sow the captured stones onto your side. Sow through your two rows, starting with the cup two ahead of the one where your last stone landed when you made the capture. This is called a **next-cup pull-across capture** and is illustrated below.

Assume the game is in progress and after several turns, you see that you can capture some of your opponent's stones to your side. Before you make your play, the board looks like this.

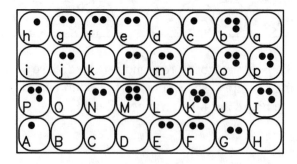

You start your next play from cup "I" and your last stone sown lands in cup "L". The board now looks like this.

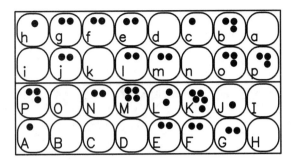

Since cup "M", following cup "L", is loaded, and cups "l" and "e" on your opponent's side are also loaded, you make a capture. Take the stones from cups "l" and "e" and sow them onto your side starting with cup "N". The board now looks like this.

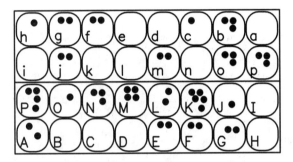

Continue sowing and capturing until the last stone you sow lands in a cup that is followed by an empty cup, ending your turn. Your opponent then makes the next play. There is no limit on the number of captures allowed on one turn.

The game ends and you win when your opponent is unable to make anymore plays, because either her front row is empty or her entire side of the board is empty or just holds singletons. When the entire board is empty, it is counted as a double win. The number of stones captured by each player is not important.

Playing in Rounds: Kisolo may be played in rounds using the rules given for Hus.

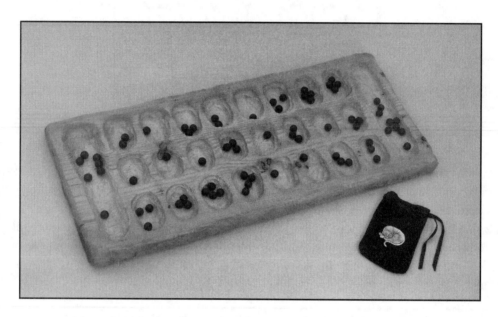

Three-row mancala board made by authors.

THREE-ROW MANCALA

THREE-ROW MANCALA is the least common type of mancala there is. In fact, until recently, the only evidence that it ever existed was a relic board found carved into an ancient Egyptian ruin. However, in the 1970s sociologist Richard Pankhurst discovered several three-row games played in the mountains of northeastern Africa.

Because there are so few documented three-row games, it is difficult to draw conclusions about them. However, a few things can be said. Three-row mancala closely resembles the two-row mancala versions played in northern Africa and the Middle East. Like these games, you sow through your opponent's cups as well as your own but never through your reservoir. In addition, three-row games are capture games, and they are generally played in rounds.

The differences between three-row mancala and other forms result from the extra row. As usual, each player owns a back row. However, the middle row is split so that each player owns the right half. The result is a path of play that twists and turns around the board. In most ways, the unconventional path has little affect on the game, making it little more than a two-row game where the end cups have been bent around. However, it does result in modifications to capturing.

Included in this chapter are two three-row games with instructions for single games as well as rounds. The first of these games is more typical of mancala, but the second has a very different form of capture and ends in a rather unexpected way.

A CROSS CAPTURE GAME

ONE-ROUND GABATA
A Basic Three-row Game

One-round Gabata is played in Ethiopia in the central highlands of Eritrea. While it is typical of African mancala, its form of capturing is reminiscent of American Cross Capture games. When played as a single game, Gabata is relatively easy, once you understand the path of play. Once you have a feel for One-round Gabata, moving on to Gabata Rounds should not be difficult.

Object: To capture more stones than your opponent by the end of the game.

Gameboard: The gameboard consists of three rows of six cups and may have, but does not require, two reservoirs at each end for storing captured stones. Each player owns the row of six cups nearest him and the three rightmost cups of the center row. Thus, your cups would be cups "A" through "I" and your opponent's cups, "a" through "i", as shown in the figure below. Since stones are not sown through the reservoir, which reservoir you own is not important. Traditionally, however, players use the reservoir on their right.

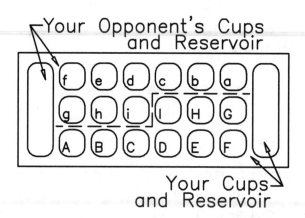

Path of Play: The path of play is shown in the figure below. Sow counterclockwise through your back row cups, "A" through "F". When you reach cup "F", sow through your middle row cups "G", "H", and then "I". From cup "I", jump to cup "a" in your opponent's back row. Sow through cups "a" through "f" and then through her middle row cups "g", "h", and "i". From cup "i", jump to cup "A" in your back row.

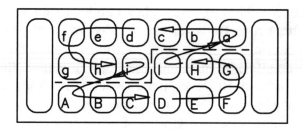

Board Setup: Fifty-four stones are required. Place three stones in each cup, leaving the reservoirs empty.

Playing:

To make a play, take all the stones from any one of your cups in either row. Sow the stones counterclockwise around the board as described above. Sow only one stone per cup, starting with the cup next to the one from which you originally took the stones.

Once you finish sowing, if the last stone you sow lands in a loaded cup anywhere on the board, continue playing. Take the stones from that cup and sow them as described above, starting with the next cup. Continue sowing in this manner until your last stone sown lands in an empty cup. This is called a continued play and is illustrated below.

Assume the game is in progress, and you are about to make your next play. Before you do, the board looks like this.

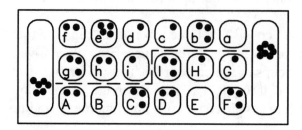

You take all the stones from cup "C" and sow them counterclockwise. The last stone sown lands in cup "F", and the board now looks like this.

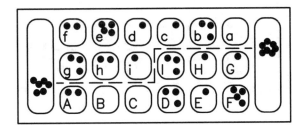

Since cup "F" was loaded, you continue playing. You pick up the stones in cup "F", including your last stone sown. You then sow them through "G", "H", and "I", starting with cup "G". From "I" you jump to your opponent's cup "a", which is also where your last stone sown lands. The stones on the board are now arranged like this.

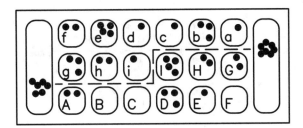

Since cup "a" was previously empty, the continued play ends.

When your last stone sown lands in an empty cup, your turn ends and your opponent makes the next play if the empty cup is

- Any of your opponent's cups ("a" through "i")
- One of your three rightmost cups in your back row ("D", "E", or "F")
- Any of your remaining cups directly across from an empty cup on your opponent's side

However, if your last stone lands in an empty cup on your side of the board that is opposite a loaded cup on your opponent's side, you capture the stones held in that cup. If the cup directly behind the one from which you captured (assuming there is one) is also loaded, you capture those stones as well. Take your captured stones, but not your last stone sown, and place them in your reservoir. Cross capturing as used in three-row games is illustrated below.

Assume the game is in progress and you see that you can capture some of your opponent's stones. Before you start your play, the board looks like this.

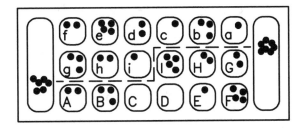

You pick up the stones from cup "A" and sow them counterclockwise. Your last stone sown lands in cup "C" in your front row. The board now looks like this.

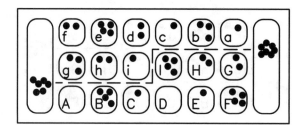

Since cup "C" was originally empty and cup "i" directly across from it held one stone, you capture that stone but not your last stone sown. Since cup "d" behind "i" is also loaded, you capture those stones as well. Take your captured stones and place them in your reservoir. The board now looks like this.

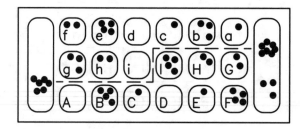

When you capture in Gabata, your turn does not necessarily end. After you take your captured stones, place your last stone sown in the next cup. If this cup was previously loaded, pick up all the stones and continue sowing as before. If the cup was previously empty, however, your turn ends unless you can make another capture. In that case, follow the rules for capturing explained above.

Continuing the example immediately above (where you made a cross capture from cup "C"), take your last stone sown from cup "C" and place it in cup "D" as shown below. Since "D" was previously empty, and it does not meet the criteria for another capture, (remember, you own cup "I" and you can not capture from your own cups), your turn ends and your opponent makes the next play.

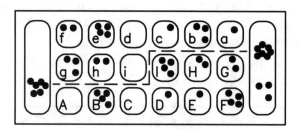

Ending:

The game ends when it is your opponent's turn and she can no longer play because:

- You made a play that cleared her side or
- She made a play that cleared her side and you can play nothing to her on your next turn

124

You capture all the stones that remain in your cups. Move them to your reservoir. However, if your opponent makes a play that clears her side, and you can play something to her on your next turn, the game continues. The player with more captured stones at the end of the game wins.

GABATA ROUNDS
The Traditional Ethiopian Game

Gabata is traditionally played in rounds with an ultimate goal similar to Mankala'h Rounds. Fifty-four stones are required. Place three stones in each cup, leaving the reservoirs empty. The object of any one round is to capture more stones than your opponent. Over a series of rounds, the ultimate goal is to hoard all of the stones or enough of them so it is not worthwhile for your opponent to continue.

Do not choose a player to begin. For the opening play of the first round, both players will play simultaneously. This play occurs only once during the game, and only during the first round. When playing simultaneously, you play by the same rules as for playing alternately, except that there is no capturing. After this play is completed, the game returns to regular alternating play where players take turns and capturing is resumed. The player who ended first on the simultaneous play makes the first alternating play.

For the first round, play as instructed above under One-round Gabata. For the second round, take the stones from your reservoir and place three in each of your cups, starting with the leftmost cup in your back row (cup "A") and moving right. If you reach cup "F" and still have stones, continue into your middle row, starting with the rightmost cup, cup "G". If you fill all your cups, return any remaining stones to your reservoir. Do <u>not</u> fill any cups on your opponent's side. (This is part of the ultimate goal of getting the stones away from your opponent.) If you can only partially fill your last cup, fill it with your remaining stones. All cups you originally owned, whether loaded or empty, remain yours and are fully active during the next round.

Start the new round with the player who won the previous round. (Some players start subsequent rounds with the player who lost the last round. This results in a lengthier game but gives the loser a better chance of winning back some of the stones.) Play as before, trying to win enough stones to fill your empty cups.

At the beginning of a new round, place your captured stones back in the cups as you did in round two. Then play as before. Repeat rounds until one player has no stones or so few that she wishes to concede.

A WEGUE GAME

ONE-ROUND SULUS NISHTAW
An Advanced Three-row Game

Sulus Nishtaw, also called Gabata, is a three-row game played in the Tigre province of Ethiopia. It is unique among mancala games, because of its unusual style of capturing stones and ending the game.

Object: To capture more stones than your opponent by the end of the game.

Gameboard: The gameboard consists of three rows of six cups. Each player owns the row of six cups nearest him and the three rightmost cups of the center row.

Board Setup: Fifty-four stones are required. Place three stones in each cup, leaving the reservoirs empty.

Playing:

To make a play, take all the stones from any one of your cups in either row, except a wegue, which will be explained below. Sow the stones counterclockwise around the board as shown in **Path of Play** under One-round Gabata. Sow only one stone per cup, starting with the cup next to the one from which you originally took the stones.

Once you finish sowing, continue playing if your last stone lands in a loaded cup anywhere on the board except

- One of your opponent's cups ("a" through "i") that originally held three stones and now holds four. (This rule is ignored on the opening play of the game.)
- An established wegue on either side of the board

Take the stones from the loaded cup and sow them as before, starting with the next cup. Continue sowing in this manner until the last stone sown lands in an empty cup or one of the cups listed above. (The continued play for a three-row board is illustrated in One-round Gabata.)

If your last stone sown lands in any empty cup, your turn ends. If it lands in one of your opponent's cups, and that cup originally held three stones and now holds four, your turn also ends. However, the cup becomes a **wegue**, and it will remain so for the entire game. Mark all wegues to help you remember where they are. (Note that only your last stone sown can create a wegue. It can not be an intermediary stone as in the case of a passing-four.)

Wegues are owned, but by whom depends on who owns the cup. You own any wegues that are established in your cups. Your opponent owns any wegues established in her cups. That you created your opponent's wegues and vice versa does not affect their ownership. (It will affect strategy, however, which will be discussed later.)

Wegues are restricted cups. You may not start a play from a wegue, although you may sow through one. You may also capture the stones held in any wegue that you own. However, you may not capture stones held in your opponent's wegues. Note that capturing stones form a wegue will not affect its status. It still remains a wegue. Also, note that due to sowing and capturing, the number of stones held in the wegue will vary throughout the game. The creation of a wegue is shown below.

Assume the game is in progress and after several turns, you see that you can create a wegue on your opponent's side. Before you start your play, the board looks like this.

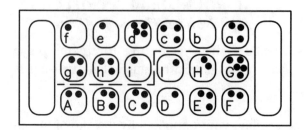

You pick up the stones from cup "G" and sow them counterclockwise through "H" and "I". Your last stone sown lands in cup "c". Since cup "c" is on your opponent's side and originally held three stones and now holds four, it becomes a wegue. Mark it to help you remember. Again, do not take any stones held in the wegue. Your turn ends and your opponent makes the next play. The board now looks like this.

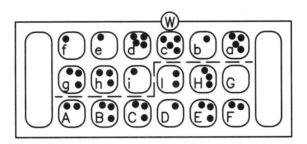

Wegues are your primary means of capturing in this game. Contrary to what you might expect, though, you do not capture from your opponent's wegues. You only capture from your own. Therefore, if your last stone sown lands in an established wegue on your side of the board, you capture. However, if it lands in an established wegue on your opponent's side, no one captures and your turn simply ends.

When you capture, you do not take all of the stones held in the wegue, however. You only capture one stone along with your last stone sown. If the wegue is empty, you still capture your last stone sown. Any stones you capture are placed in your reservoir. You then take another turn, starting with any of your cups that is not a wegue. Capturing from wegues is illustrated below.

Assume the game is in progress and that cup "C" (on your side) was made a wegue on a previous turn. (Remember that you may not capture from a cup until it becomes a wegue.) After several turns, you see that you can capture one of the stones held in cup "C". Before you start your play, the board looks like this.

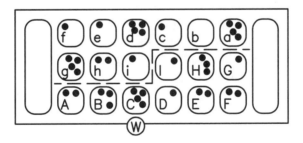

You pick up the stones from cup "A" and sow them counterclockwise. Your last stone sown lands in cup "C".

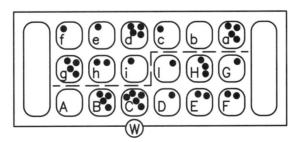

Since cup "C" is a wegue, you capture one of its stones plus your last stone sown. Take the stones and place them in your reservoir. After removing the captured stones, the board looks like this.

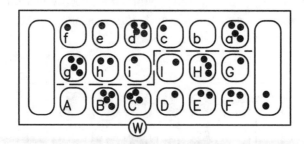

Once you have removed your captured stones, take another turn, starting from any one of your cups that are not wegues. Note that you may not start your play from cup "C", because although you captured some of the stones, "C" remains a wegue.

Ending:

The game ends when it is your opponent's turn and she can no longer play because her side consists entirely of wegues, empty cups, or a combination. Then you and she both take any stones held in wegues, but not the ones on your side of the board. Instead, take the stones held in the wegues on your opponent's side of the board. Move them to your respective reservoirs. If any of your cups that are not wegues also hold stones, take these and place them in your reservoir. The player with more captured stones wins.

Variations:

Restricted leftmost cup

This variation favors your opponent. Play as described above, except that you may not start a new play from your leftmost cup in your back row (cup "A") unless it contains more than three stones. In this way, it is more likely to become a wegue, one from which you will have difficulty capturing the stones because of its location.

Notes on Strategy:

Because of its unconventional form of capturing and ending, the strategy of Sulus Nishtaw is somewhat confusing. Here are some tips. First, remember that you create wegues on your opponent's side of the board, but you capture from the wegues on your side. This may seem backward, but it makes sense if you consider the way the game ends: you keep any stones held in your opponent's wegues, giving her the stones in yours.

Second, as you play, try to establish a balance between wegues and regular cups. You need a few wegues on your side to give you opportunities to capture stones and increase your winnings during the game. However, too many wegues may reduce your options for starting a play (since you may not start a play from a wegue). It also increases your opponent's chances of capturing stones from your wegues at the end of the game.

Third, keep in mind that it is easier to capture stones from wegues established in your rightmost cups than your leftmost cups. This is due to the counterclockwise direction of play. In addition, it is easier to capture from wegues that are spread out rather than sequential. Of course, because of continued play and the fact that wegues are created by your opponent, wegue placement is difficult to control. However, by watching which cups hold three stones, you have some control.

SULUS NISHTAW ROUNDS
The Traditional Ethiopian Game

When played in rounds, Sulus Nishtaw is reminiscent of Adi. This is because in Sulus Nishtaw you want to disable your opponent by capturing all or most of her cups. Thus, the object of each round is to capture as many stones as possible. Over a series of rounds, the ultimate goal is to leave your opponent unable to play, because you have captured most or all of the cups on the board.

For the first round, play as described under One-round Sulus Nishtaw. For the second round, begin by removing all of your wegue markers. There are no wegues at the beginning of any new round. Then take the stones from your reservoir and place three in each of your cups, starting with your leftmost cup in your back row, cup "A", and moving right. If you reach cup "F" and still have stones left, continue into your middle row, starting with the rightmost cup, cup "G", and moving left.

If you fill all your cups and have stones left over, continue onto your opponent's side. Fill her cups with three stones, starting with cup "a" and moving counterclockwise. If you end up with fewer than three stones, combine those with your opponent's remaining stones to fill the last cup.

Any cups you fill with two or three stones, including those on your opponent's side, are yours for the round. All remaining cups belong to your opponent, including any cups you were able to fill with only one stone. If you find it difficult to keep track of the cups you own, place a marker beside them to help you remember. Be sure that you use something different from your wegue markers, since some cups may have two markers. Start the new round with the person who has fewer cups.

At the beginning of a new round, place your captured stones back in the cups as you did in round two. Cups lost during the previous round can be taken back if enough stones were captured. Then play as before.

Rounds are repeated until one player is left with fewer than two stones and therefore has no cups. However, once either player is down to three cups, it is almost impossible to recover and players usually agree to end the game. The player who owns more cups wins the game.

BIBLIOGRAPHY

Agostini, Franco, and Nicola Alberto De Carlo. *Intelligence Games.* Simon & Schuster, New York, 1985.

Ainslie, Tom. *Ainslie's Complete Hoyle.* Simon and Schuster, New York, 1975.

Arnold, Peter (ed.). *The Book of Games.* Viscount Books, New York, 1985.

Arnold, Peter (ed.). *Board and Table Games.* Exeter Books, New York, 1975.

Bell, R. C. *Board and Table Games from Many Civilizations.* Dover Publications, New York, 1979.

Bell, R. C. *The Boardgame Book.* Exeter Books, New York, 1983.

Bell, R. C. *Discovering Old Board Games.* Shire Publications, U.K., 1973.

Botermans, Jack, Tony Burrett, Pieter van Delft, and Carla van Splentereen. *The World of Games.*

Facts on File, New York & Oxford, 1989.

Braunholtz, H. J. "The Game of Mweso in Uganda." *Man*, Vol. 31, 1931.

Chaplin, J. H. "A Note on Mancala Games in Northern Rhodesia." *Man*, December 1956.

Collins, G. N. "Kboo, a Liberian Game." *National Geographic Magazine*, 1910.

Cruickshank, J. G. Letter to the editor. *Man*, Vol. 29, No. 141, 1929.

Crane, Louise. *African Games of Strategy: African Outreach Series, No. 2.* University of Illinois, Champaign, IL, 1982.

Deledicq, A. and A. Popova. *Wari et Solo.* CEDIC, Paris, 1977.

Driberg, J. H. "The Game of Choro or Pereauni." *Man*, September 1927 & October 1927.

Durai, H. G. "Pallanguli: A South Indian Game." *Man*, November 1928.

Goren, Charles H. *Goren's Hoyle Encyclopedia of Games.* Chancellor hall, LTD. New York, 1961.

Grunfeld, Frederic V. (ed.). *Games of the World.* Holt, Rinehart, and Winston, New York, 1975.

Hellier, M. "Notes on the Malay Game 'Jongkak'." *Journal* of *the Royal Asiatic Society* (Straits Branch), No. 49, December 1907.

Herskovits, M. J. "Adjiboto, an African Game of the Bush-Negroes of Dutch Guiana." *Man,* Vol. 29, 1929.

Hopson, Dr. Darlene Powell, and Dr. Derek S. Hopson, with Thomas Clavin, *Juba This and Juba That.* Simon and Schuster.

Lane, E. W. *The Manners and Customs of the Modern Egyptians.* J.M. Dent & Sons, London, 1890.

Museum and Archive of Games. "Count and Capture Games." University of Waterloo, Ontario, Canada, 1977.

Pankhurst, R. "Gabata and Related Board Games of Ethiopia and the Horn of Africa." *Ethiopia Observer*, Vol. XIV, No. 3, 1971.

Prior, Jennifer. *The Games of Africa.* Harper Festival, New York, 1994.

Russ, Larry. *The Complete Mancala Games Book.* Marlowe & Company, New York, 1995.

Scarne, John. *Scarne's Encyclopedia of Games.* Harper & Row, New York, 1973

INDEX